UP AGAINST THE WALL
MOTHERF✳✳KER

UP AGAINST THE WALL MOTHERF**KER

A MEMOIR OF THE '60S, WITH NOTES FOR NEXT TIME

OSHA NEUMANN

SEVEN STORIES PRESS
NEW YORK • LONDON • MELBOURNE • TORONTO

Seven Stories Press
140 Watts Street
New York, NY 10013
www.sevenstories.com

In Canada: Publishers Group Canada, 559 College Street, Suite 402, Toronto, ON M6G 1A9

In the UK: Turnaround Publisher Services Ltd., Unit 3, Olympia Trading Estate, Coburg Road, Wood Green, London N22 6TZ

In Australia: Palgrave Macmillan, 15–19 Claremont Street, South Yarra, VIC 3141

College professors may order examination copies of Seven Stories Press titles for a free six-month trial period. To order, visit http://www.sevenstories.com/textbook or send a fax on school letterhead to (212) 226-1411.

Book design by Jon Gilbert

Library of Congress Cataloging-in-Publication Data

Neumann, Osha, 1939–
Up against the wall motherf**ker : a memoir of the '60s, with notes for next time / Osha Neumann. — Seven Stories Press 1st ed.
    p. cm.
Includes bibliographical references.
ISBN 978-1-58322-849-4 (pbk.)
1. Up Against the Wall Motherfuckers (Gang)—History. 2. Neumann, Osha, 1939–
3. Gangs—United States. I. Title. II. Title: Up against the wall motherfucker.
HV6439.U5N48 2008
364.1092—dc22
[B]

                                      2008032958

Printed in the USA.

9 8 7 6 5 4 3 2 1

CONTENTS

PREFACE

In 1967, I became a founding member of an anarchist street gang called Up Against the Wall Motherfuckers, an unexpected career move for a nice Jewish boy with an MA in history from Yale.

We called ourselves the Motherfuckers. We saw ourselves as urban guerrillas swimming in the countercultural sea of freaks and dropouts (we didn't like the media term "hippies") who had swarmed to the cheap-rent tenements of the Lower East Side of New York. Those young dropouts were our base, and we attempted to organize them for total revolution through rallies, free feasts, raucous community meetings, and a steady stream of mimeographed flyers. Against the vapid spaciness of "flower power" we proclaimed the need for "Armed Love." Our rhetoric was inflammatory and often violent.

We gave speeches and wrote manifestos, but above all we believed in propaganda of the deed. We engaged in constant confrontations with the police. We would start riots, get arrested, start another one to protest our arrests, and get arrested again. After one of my arrests I appeared before a judge who called me "a cross between Rap Brown and Hitler." I greeted his summation of my character with a mixture of pride and shame. I felt like a kid whose scary Halloween costume has been more successful than he intended.

As a child I'd imagined I was destined to become a professor and write books. My parents were German Jewish refugees from the Nazis. My father was Franz Neumann, the author of *Behemoth*, a seminal study of fascist Germany. His best friend was Herbert Marcuse. Herbert's most famous books, *Eros and Civilization* and *One-Dimensional Man*, are philosophical critiques of civilization and its discontents that rejected the rigid analytic framework of dogmatic Marxism. His writing and speeches provided theoretical legitimization to the unorthodox countercultural movements of the Sixties and made him something of a father figure to a generation that generally distrusted anyone over thirty.

Herbert moved into our house after his wife Sophie died of cancer in 1951. While living with us he continued a secret affair with my mother that had begun sometime earlier. Inge, my mother, was a brilliant woman, who sacrificed her own ambitions in order to do what was expected at the time of a mother and faculty wife. Her marriage to Franz was not a happy one. I suspect that in her unhappiness, she vented her frustration on me. We fought endlessly.

I grew up in a Manichean world. Fascism was the expression of the irrational; reason was its opposite. The distinction was clear and unambiguous. By the time I reached junior high school I had already reached the conclusion that our home was the clean well-lighted citadel of reason and I was an irrational foul-smelling insect befouling it. I became obsessive and introverted.

In becoming a Motherfucker I renounced my commitment to ordered discourse, the traffic in abstractions, respect for explanations, the demand for coherence, and the subordination of impulse and emotion—all of which I thought of as characteristic of a life committed to reason. I grew fierce in my scorn for theory. I felt most alive when running in the streets with no thoughts in my head but where the cops were and how to avoid them. But my apostasy was never complete. As the Mafia don longs for respectability, as the dealer in prostitutes and drugs can be the staunchest proponent of family values, so I, the rebellious child of reason, longed for the respectable cloak of rationality and pledged allegiance to reason even as I plunged headlong into the irrational.

I'm no longer a Motherfucker and childhood is a distant memory, but I still think of reason somewhat vaguely as a universally applicable method for determining truth and validating judgments. I have never been really sure what it is, but I appeal to it anyway.

Reason or revelation. How else do we decide what's right and wrong? Some of us appeal to the one, some of us to the other. But both have their problems. God has too many spokespeople, each certain he's the chosen mouthpiece, none making a credible argument in the age of cell phones, black holes, concentration camps, weapons of mass destruction, mad cow disease, and reality television. Reason has got some of the same problems God has: too many people appealing to it for too many different purposes. Far too often the powers that be who ask us to be reasonable and not rock the boat act as if they were stark raving mad, hell bent on incinerating their enemies, polluting nature, promoting inequality, and grabbing as much loot for themselves as possible. What they call progress is destruction. What they call democracy is subjugation. The tools for the alleviation of want are turned into the means for its perpetuation.

"Reason has always existed, but not always in a rational form," wrote a twenty-year-old Karl Marx.[1] I would like to think that the Motherfuckers represented reason "but not in a rational form." Although I have written the confession of a Motherfucker, I am the least motherfuckery of Motherfuckers. I have been quite tamed by time, and to tell the truth I was probably not much of a motherfucker even back then, though I put on a pretty good show. What I have to confess are mainly bad thoughts and crimes of the imagination.

* * *

Long gone are the Sixties, in whose rollicking tumult I found for a while meaning and purpose. We were children then and now we are grown, though there are those of us who remain, even today, somewhat puzzled by the process. Some of us have not wanted to look back, and some of us have looked back compulsively. I have been more in the former camp than the latter. But forgetting is neither an option nor desirable. In 1973, Elinor Langer wrote a reflection on her experiences in the Sixties called *Notes for Next Time*. It's a good title, clearly implying the intent to sight a firm pragmatic course towards the future based on a charting of past coordinates. But it's now been over thirty years since she wrote her notes and "next time" hasn't happened. Rather than experiencing another outpouring of revolutionary enthusiasm, we are locked in a dogged fight against reaction. Things are going from bad to worse. The world is not a better place for all our efforts.

What went wrong? Why now this regression? Why do the most atavistic forms of consciousness flourish in the midst of modernity? Why does reason appear powerless in the face of unreason? What should we have done differently? What is to be done now? In the Thirties, my parents fled the Nazis and spent much of their subsequent lives thinking about these questions. In the Sixties I fled my parents, plunged into Motherfuckering, and emerged from the aborted revolution of the Sixties with the same questions still unanswered. They remain unanswered today. And they remain just as urgent.

* * *

Memory is a leaky vessel. Cargo falls overboard, and sinks into the sea of forgetfulness. What remains is contaminated. The bilge water of false memories seeps through the packaging. Rats gnaw through the ropes that bind together moments of time. Ordered sequences of events, neatly packaged at the onset of the journey, break open and scatter helter-skelter about the hold of the ship. Disparate moments of our public and private lives are jumbled together. The original bill of lading is lost. Salvage is incomplete at best.

My salvage effort has been aided by conversations with surviving Motherfuckers. I am grateful to them for taking the time to talk to me, and would acknowledge them by name, but some do and some do not want to be associated with our nefarious past. They have gone on to make lives for themselves as lawyers, shamans, poets, midwives, farmers, jewelers, wilderness guides and environmental activists. I thank them all anonymously. Although we were a small group, we did not all share the same experience. I've pieced together our story as best I can. Where our memories differ, I've said so.

Thanks also to all who participated in and organized the 2008 gathering to commemorate the fortieth anniversary of the takeover of Columbia University. Out of our extended hash and rehash of the events of 1968 emerged a picture, which, though not entirely coherent or without contradiction, is infinitely better than any we could have painted on our own with the frayed brush of our failing memory.

There have been many who have helped and encouraged me along the way. Nore Lee first encouraged me to take on the arduous task of seeking a publisher. Kosta Bagakis and Barbara Epstein were constantly encouraging, as have been Elinor Langer, John McMillian, and Clayton Patterson. I thank my daughters, Rachel and Emma, for inspiring me with hope and continuing to love me despite my propensity to embarrass them with TMI [too much information]. Thanks also to Yeshi Neumann and Alan Steinbach.

Finally I thank my wife, Arisika Razak. Some of what I have written she finds deeply disturbing. When she first read the manuscript of his book she considered divorcing me because of my insistence on sharing the perverse sexual fantasies that accompanied me through my days of rage as a Motherfucker. She asked me, "Why would a woman who has been raped or molested want to read that stuff? What are you trying to prove?" She is convinced that no moat is wide enough to prevent the fantasy of sexual violence from fulfilling itself on the bodies of women. I answered that something of the energy that went into my fantasies also went into my politics. That's important to know and say. She's not persuaded. Nor can I persuade her to value the proclamations of human rights by white men, who treated her ancestors as less than human. "Do you think the slaves were waiting for Jefferson to explain to them the value of freedom?" she asks. Arisika has continued to love me through our arguments. She's been patient as I slowly awaken to the realization that unconsciously I had been imagining a reader for my writing who was white and male. She's given me time to make the required adjustments. Her love has been a precious gift for which I am enormously grateful.

EXILES

I was born in New York in 1939. Inge and Franz named me Thomas after Thomas Mann and Thomas Jefferson, a twentieth century German novelist and an eighteenth century American slaveholder who, despite the contradictions of their lives, articulated Enlightenment values that were antithetical to fascism. In 1969 when I was living in New Mexico with the remnants of the Motherfuckers, I changed my name to "Osha," after an inconspicuous herb that grows in the rocky cut backs of the roads that run through the Sangre de Christo Mountains. It has a long pungent taproot and is sacred to the Pueblo and Apache Indians of the area. They smoke it and wear it about their necks to ward off rattlesnakes. Boiled, it makes a tea that clears the mind and sinuses and helps induce abortions.

My parents emigrated to the United States three years before my birth. They were part of a Great Migration of intellectuals and artists who fled Germany with the rise of fascism. Settling into their new homeland with various degrees of ease and enthusiasm, they formed loose communities of exiles centered in New York and Los Angeles. They included the writers Thomas Mann and Bertolt Brecht; musicians Kurt Weill and Arnold Schoenberg; scientists Albert Einstein and Edward Teller; psychoanalysts Erik Erikson, Bruno Bettelheim, and Wilhelm Reich; and social theorists such as my fathers, and their colleagues from the Frankfurt Institute for Social Research, Theodor Adorno and Max Horkheimer. Today the Institute would probably be called a "think tank." The intellectuals connected with it were, by and large, independent of party affiliation. Pessimistic about the ability of the left to prevent the rise of fascism in the waning days of the Weimar Republic, they strove to rethink Marxism and develop a critical theory that would survive the collapse of Europe into barbarism. They read Freud and reread Hegel. They wrote about music and literature as well as economics, sociology, and philosophy.

A year after I was born the Neumanns and the Marcuses moved to Washington, where Franz and Herbert worked for the Office of Strategic Services, the predecessor of the CIA, doing intelligence on Germany. After the war, Franz got a job as a professor of political science at Columbia University and Herbert went to work at the Russian Research Center. Franz and Inge bought a comfortable two-story house on Arlington Avenue in Riverdale, the upscale part of the Bronx that borders the Hudson River. On the opposite side of the street was the Nip Nichen Tennis club, which was rumored to exclude Jews and Blacks.

I have a childhood memory of sitting, curled up on a comfortable sofa in the corner of the living room of my parents' home on Arlington Avenue. Through the door to the dining room, I can see my father and his friends, Herbert among them, sitting at the dinner table. They are engaged in an intense discussion about the state of the world. Silverware clatters on the china. Odors of the roast my mother prepared for dinner drift over to my nest of pillows, accompanied by the sound of the grownups' conversation. They argue in the heavily accented English of newly exiled German Jews. Herbert lights his pipe. A dispute breaks out over the meaning of a word or the date of some historical event. Herbert gets up, goes to the bookcase and pulls out a volume of the 13th edition of the *Encyclopedia Britannica*, or perhaps William Langer's one volume *Encyclopedia of World History*. He returns to the dinner table loudly proclaiming he will prove his point. The conversation continues. This person is a "Dumkopf (literally a dumbhead); that one is an "Arschloch" (an asshole). Politicians are invariably "fascist beasts." Herbert quotes Shakespeare, whom, he is fond of saying, is "much better in the original German." Laughter and demands to pass the coffee and the bottle of Schnapps punctuate the argument. I curl deeper into the sofa, reassured by the sound of the grownups' voices, that knowing is possible and therefore the world could be made safe. I had no doubt that my parents had escaped the Holocaust because they correctly analyzed the situation in which they lived, and so did not fall prey to dangerous illusions. The ability to think had saved their lives.

At a very early age I came to the conclusion that my parents understood everything. From their dinner table conversations, I acquired my fundamental commitment to antifascism. I concluded that my birthright was an all encompassing theory, Marxism, which sought to determine, in each historical period, the forces which represent humanity's hope for liberation and a just ordering of human affairs. Fascism was a mighty upsurge of irrationality, a release of corrupt desires from the bounds of moderation and reason, the triumph of stupidity and conformity over intelligence and independent thought. The struggle against fascism was the struggle of the oppressed against the oppressor, and of reason against irrationality. Auschwitz was the embodiment of irrationality. The embodiment of rationality was the scholarly community of exiled Marxist Jewish intellectuals who were my parents' friends and colleagues.

* * *

To be antifascist was to be committed to reason. Passion, chaos, muscularity were all suspect. Reason took sides in the battleground of history. It was the guiding thread linking each succeeding generation of rebels who struggled to birth a world in which the few would no longer benefit from the misery of the many. Reason had no country but the truth, no allegiance but to equality and justice. The universality of reason, its refusal of parochial boundaries, provided the surest basis for the solidarity of the many who must unite if the struggle to make a better world was to succeed.

In my parents' record cabinet, below the Mozart, the Schubert and the Beethoven, was a half empty shelf with a few stray records of folk music—Burl Ives and John Jacob Niles, Paul Robeson of course, and a small LP with a red cover, *Songs of the Spanish Civil War*. Those songs, sung primarily in German and Spanish, enthralled me. I learned them by heart, bellowing out "*Viva la Quince Brigada rum dada rum dada rumdadda rum*," imitating the accents of the singers as I imitated to the best of my ability Paul Robeson's deep baritone and John Jacob Niles high counter tenor. Through those songs I caught a glimpse of a passionate and worthy time, of deeds that captured the imagination. Our side had lost, but from the trenches dug deep into Spanish soil by the singers of those songs, hope rose like a rush of startled birds into the night sky. I imagined sweaty exhausted men, resting on the hard earth beneath a night sky full of stars. Their rifles cradled in their arms, they inhaled air perfumed with the odor of wine and olives. Drifting off to sleep, they listened to the sound of a guitar and a singer softly singing:

And just because he's human
He doesn't want a pistol in his back.
He wants no servants under him
And no lord over his head
So left one two, so left one two
To the workers we must go
March on march on in the United Front
For you are a worker too.[2]

In my fantasy, a bridge of theory connected the bloody battle for Spain and the academic life of my parents. Men went to fight in Spain because of a set of beliefs about the world derived from the work of thinkers, like my parents, deeply devoted to making sense of the world. With such fantasies I struggled, not entirely successfully, to reconcile reason's strict demand to prioritize thinking over doing with the unruly energies of my corrupt, insistent body.

I had always thought of my home as an enclave of intellect. My parents' life was for me the model of a life of reason. That model included a clean, comfortable, well ordered home; wives who cooked well and took care of the children; and teaching positions for the men in prestigious universities.

Here in the Bronx, rationality had found a safe haven. There was only one problem. From as early as I can remember, the surface tranquility of our bourgeois family life was broken by a fearsome conflict between my mother and me. I now suspect that her discontent with me was the expression of her frustration at having to raise a child without support in a strange country, compounded by resentment at having to give up an academic career, dissatisfaction with the role of faculty wife, and the stress of her secret liaison with Herbert.

Inge was ten years younger than Franz, taller, and to my mind, more robust and physically formidable. By contrast I remember him as somewhat rotund and soft. He was bald except for a ring of black hair in the back, myopic, and hard of hearing. He peered out at the world from behind thick glasses with wire frames and wore a hearing aid attached to a black plastic battery case strapped to his chest. I do not recall his voice ever being raised in anger.

If Inge and Herbert made love under my father's nose—and mine—I suspected nothing. I caught no glimpse of fleeting embraces. If Inge and Franz fought, they did so quietly or when I was not around.

All the adults had separate bedrooms. They all managed their lives so that there would be dinners without arguments, and mornings without tears and recriminations. But my mother and I could not manage. We carried on a prolonged and desperate struggle, in which both of us were losers. I was sure I was to blame, and that what was blameworthy in me was something over which I had no control—my very being.

Franz took no part in my epic battles with my mother. In all matters that pertained to my upbringing, he deferred to her entirely. Outside the home, among his students, he inspired awe and admiration. One described him as having a mind "like an incandescent bulb which, although it had burned away his hair, his sight, and his hearing, continued to exert a fascination on all . . . [he] encountered."[3] Inside the home he was timid and submissive. He would retreat to his book-lined study, where I remember him sitting for hours on a couch doing the Sunday *New York Times* crossword puzzle.

Franz was ineffective as my defender, but my happiest childhood memories are of sitting on his lap while he read me wonderful adventure stories. The best, *Treasure Island*, *The Last of the Mohicans*, and *Kidnapped*, had illustrations by N. C. Wyeth that remain with me to this day: a pirate, climbing up the rigging with a knife clenched in his teeth, an Indian wrestling with a buckskin-clad frontiersman on the edge of a precipice.

My father took me on his lap and together we escaped the wrath of my mother, until, one day, she decided that I was not learning to read because I preferred to be read to. She forbade Franz to read to me, banished me from his lap, and bought me glasses. I hated them. Imprisoned in glasses that bounced on my nose when I ran and fell off when I turned somersaults, I felt like a horse that had been haltered and taken from his pasture to wear forever bridle and blinder.

The conflict with my mother centered on dirt and disorder. Either I was unusually filthy or my mother was unusually obsessed. My mother's constant complaints nurtured my sense of personal vileness. All my bodily impulses were bad. I was the turd laid in the living room of reason, the damned spot on the rug that would not be cleansed. In a world divided between fascists and antifascists I became: the dirty little Jew as fascist.

In a world divided between fascists and antifascists I became the dirty little Jew as fascist.

SECRETS AND CATASTROPHES

When I was about eight or nine, it occurred to me that my parents, together with all the other adults in my life, had entered into a great conspiracy whose purpose was to conceal from me something very important about myself. I could never find out what it was, but I was sure that if I ever discovered their secret, my view of myself and the world would be completely altered. Like a tail sprouting out my backside, whatever was being concealed was obvious to everyone but me. The baker, the butcher, my teacher, my babysitter all saw it and pretended it wasn't there. They smiled at me and treated me as if I was completely normal. But I wasn't.

I never took this fantasy completely seriously, nor did I ever completely discount it. I know now my parents had many secrets. Family and friends had died in the Holocaust. I learned later from my aunt Susan that Franz's mother died in Buchenwald. And perhaps it was my aunt Harriet who told me that Inge's mother, driven to despair as the Nazis consolidated their hold on her crumbling world, committed suicide by gassing herself in the kitchen oven. But my parents never spoke to me of such matters. They shielded me from the past. And they shielded me from the present. My brother Michael, who was born seven years after me, remembers something—a glimpse of intimacy, the sound of lovemaking just beyond the range of hearing, an exchange of looks—that alerted him to the concealed affair between Inge and Herbert. Whether or not my father knew about the affair I will never know.

I suspect now that some intuition of these secrets lay at the heart of my fantasy. No one now living knows exactly when Inge and Herbert's affair might have started, and so I have never been completely clear who my father is. As a result I tend to split the difference. I vacillate between thinking of myself as having a single father or two. My brother has my father's rather modest nose. I have Herbert's prominent proboscis, and his gray blue eyes. The timber of my voice is identical to that of Peter, Herbert and Sophie's son. We sound alike on the telephone.

Very early, in the bosom of the family, a child learns that appearance and reality diverge. Once learned the lesson is not forgotten. I still think of truth as hidden, and believe The System—capitalist, patriarchal, racist, however you wish to characterize it—to be a living lie from which the mask must be torn by acts of radical transgression. I know that I am not alone in the conviction that the world is fundamentally not as it appears. Distrust of what we are told runs deep and wide like an underground river beneath the jolly acquiescence of our daily lives.

* * *

Until I was fourteen I believed, as most children do, that my family was a permanent and immutable structure. I had my mother and my father, just as I had my nose, my mouth, and my eyes. And then, as so often happens, a series of catastrophes changed everything.

It was the middle of June. I was home, marooned between school and summer camp. Franz was away traveling and lecturing in Europe. In the middle of the night I was awakened by the sound of my mother crying in her room on the floor below me. The next day at breakfast, her voice shaking with anger, she informed me that my father was having an affair with one of his graduate students. She and my father were separating and would get a divorce.

No adult had ever talked to me about the personal life of grown-ups. My mother's brief announcement was an astounding breach of protocol. What did it mean for me? Would I ever see my father again? I could not even formulate the questions. Nor could I guess that the mother who stood before me, wronged and abandoned, was also the mistress of my father's best friend.

Three months passed. I was again up in my room, this time getting ready to go to school, when my mother called me downstairs. She was standing next to the stove in the kitchen. She asked me to sit down and poured me a glass of milk. She had something important to tell me. I waited. The glass of milk sat in front of me on the table. Then she told me that my father had been killed in a car accident in Switzerland. He had been traveling with his good friends, the Altmans. The car in which they were all traveling had unaccountably gone over the edge on a mountain road. Everyone had died instantly. My father had been in the back seat. She made a point of that. He had not committed suicide.

I remember thinking: I should feel something. But I felt nothing. I gathered up my books and took the bus to school. I came back. If we had any further conversations on the subject, I do not remember them. My father disappeared from my life as if he had never been there.

I had totally misjudged the situation. He had desire. He was not a eunuch. He was flesh. By leaving my mother he had regained his body. Fear of my mother's wrath had not deterred him. He had made his escape. And then, like a slave who flees the plantation only to fall into a swamp and drown, he had paid the price of freedom with his life. I was proud of him and I was angry with him for abandoning me. But above all, I was numbed by the events he had set in motion.

The message I got was clear. There is no escape. The price of freedom is death. And part of me died when he died. I suffered a kind of psychic spinal cord injury. I could think, but I couldn't feel what I was thinking about. I gave up all hope. And I have struggled ever since to regain it.

One evening, some weeks after my mother's announcement, I was in my room, trying to finish my homework, when suddenly I began to cry. Tears streamed down my face onto the book that lay open on the desk in front of me. They came out of nowhere. I had not been thinking about my father. I had not been feeling sad. It was as if a piece of plumbing had burst. I sat in front of my open book, the tears kept coming, and I continued to feel nothing in particular.

I endured the memorial service at Columbia University. It had nothing to do with me. I was forced to put on a tie and sit in the front row and accept awkward condolences from grownups who were utter strangers. I had no one to turn to—certainly not my mother, who shortly thereafter, in what some people considered unseemly haste, married Herbert. Perhaps worried that I would share their disapproval, my mother informed me that the marriage had been planned before my father died, that Herbert had told him, and that he had given his unqualified blessing to the union.

Herbert and Inge were married before a justice of the peace. Afterwards, at a crowded reception at Inge's sister's apartment on the upper west side of Manhattan, I watched as they embraced and heard my mother say "kiss me," and he did. To my astonishment, they both seemed to enjoy it. I don't remember my mother and Franz exchanging a single sign of affection. They did not embrace in my presence. This was the first and last and only display of physical affection I recollect witnessing between any of my parents.

I spent the years remaining before my departure for college, sunk in the contemplation of my own misery and struggling with an emerging sexuality, which grew stunted and misshapen in the infertile soil of my self-loathing. When I was fifteen I read Dostoevsky's *Notes from the Underground* and imagined myself the underground man reveling in degradation.

> The more aware I was of 'the highest and the best,' as we used to say, the deeper I sank into my slime, and the more capable I became of immersing myself completely in it . . . It was as if this was my normal condition, not a disease or a festering sore in me, so that finally I lost even the desire to struggle against the spell . . . I didn't believe the same thing could happen to other people, and so I have kept the secret to myself my whole life. I was ashamed. . . .[4]

I remember thinking: Dostoevsky wrote about miserable, pathetic, humiliated, mediocre people. But he was a great man. A genius. Perhaps I could be the first truly mediocre man to give an authentic account of mediocrity.

I discovered Dostoevsky and masturbation at about the same time—an unfortunate conjunction. I was so ignorant about matters pertaining to my penis that the first time I masturbated—lying in a warm bath, absentmindedly fondling myself—I had no idea what was happening and assumed that somehow, by fondling myself, I had prematurely released urine that was not fully digested.

Despite the collapse of my parent's marriage, I still perceived grownups as defined by their ability to subordinate the passions of the body to the guiding hand of reason. But my body rebelled, clouding my mind with perverse desire. Reason was not what guided my hand to my penis. My two fathers, Franz and Herbert, and my mother were aristocrats of the intellect. I was their crippled offspring.

Reason spoke with a German accent. It was Jewish, and it was out of place in America, a stranger in a land it could never make its own. I associated it with decorum, privacy and muted sensation. Sublimation of desire was the price of a decent life. The fascists were the ones without restraint. Walking home from school I passed shopkeepers, delivery people, plumbers, bus drivers, cops, hairdressers, mothers pushing strollers, old men sitting on park benches. I passed through their world like a stranger, burdened with envy of their direct, unmediated contact with reality, and at the same time believing that, being deficient in understanding, they were doomed to a lesser form of existence than that enjoyed by my parents. I worried that if I did not succeed in becoming a professor at a university, I would be similarly doomed. In so far as I wished to participate in life directly like "ordinary" people, I wished my own destruction.

* * *

After Herbert and Inge's marriage, Herbert accepted a job in the philosophy department at Brandeis University and we moved to Newton, Massachusetts, a decorous suburb of Boston. We lived on a street lined with Sycamore trees. The lawns on both sides were carefully tended. Home life went on much as it had in the Bronx. My mother cooked and maintained the house. Herbert's colleagues came over periodically for dinner.

One evening, a few months before I went away to college, I borrowed my mother's car to go out on a date with Ellen

Maslow, the daughter of Abraham Maslow, who was at the time the Chair of the Psychology Department at Brandeis and the exponent of a humanistic psychology of "self-actualization," which Herbert thought of as total drivel. I was driving home from my date, daydreaming to the music on the radio, when I rear-ended a car stopped ahead of me at an intersection. I ran over to see if the other driver was all right. She was resting her head on the steering wheel. In a dazed voice she told me she had hit her head on the windshield and felt dizzy. I was sick with fear. I have only a vague recollection of what happened next. Police arrived and took a report. The woman was still sitting in the car when they allowed me to leave. I drove home and ran into the house, fighting back tears. Inge and Herbert were sitting side by side on the sofa in the living room. My voice shaking, I told them what had happened. I wanted to be comforted. I wanted to be told everything would be ok. But Inge said nothing and Herbert, putting down his book, told me that in his opinion the accident was an unconscious expression of my anger against my mother.

I was overwhelmed by a sudden and uncontrollable fury. I picked up a heavy alabaster bowl that was sitting on a coffee table in front of them and hurled it against the wall above Herbert's head. It shattered into pieces. I stormed out of the house. I was angry and quite pleased with myself at the same time.

The target of my first and only childhood expression of overt rage was the beloved father figure of the New Left, who anointed a generation of rebels with the balm of theory. But he had not read to me on his lap. He was not a loving father. He was a usurper. I would not be his intellectual problem to be analyzed. For years I kept fragments of that bowl, carrying it with me when I moved from one place to another, thinking I would repair it some day. Then I lost them. I no longer throw alabaster bowls, but in that moment was born in me a deep attraction to the transgressive act as revelation and release.

* * *

I graduated from Newton High School in 1957 and was accepted at Swarthmore, a small Quaker college eleven miles outside of Philadelphia.

The tiny town of Swarthmore was prim and lily-white. The sale of liquor was banned inside the city limits. It didn't have a movie theater or a decent cafeteria or any place you could buy a proper Philadelphia Cheese steak. The campus was a botanical garden. World famous rhododendrons grew by the banks of Crum Creek. I was miserable. The last thing I needed was cloistered tranquility. I yearned to be in touch with what I imagined to be real life, the life of working, pleasure seeking, flesh and blood human beings. I felt separated from the real by a vast stagnant sea. I wanted the real to reel me in, to pull me from my obsessions and compulsions.

I lived in a boys' dormitory at the outskirts of the campus. My first roommate was heavyset, cheery, neat and clean. I found him repellent. One evening I noticed a sliding wooden door at the end of a corridor. I pried it open and discovered an abandoned freight elevator. By operating its rope pulleys, I could move it up and down between floors. I brought my bedding and a chair into the elevator and created a hiding place for myself. There was a bare electric bulb in the ceiling. There were no windows. Night was the same as day. I could hear the sounds of people coming and going in the corridors. No one knew I was there. I literally inhabited the woodwork. I had become a living, breathing Dostoevsky character. My compulsive self-consciousness made it difficult to approach any of the girls to whom I was attracted. I was sure they would see through me immediately to the secret masturbator. On one rare occasion, I persuaded one of them—she has since become a famous feminist historian—to come to my room. We necked heavily. I was very aroused. When she left, I put on a recording of a Mozart quartet. I wasn't sure whether, having experienced carnal passion, the higher sublimated pleasures of art would still appeal to me.

I spent my junior year abroad at the London School of Economics. I didn't go to many classes, but I heard Peggy Seeger and Ewen McCall sing whaling songs in a little upstairs West End club. Ewen cupped his hand over his ear to hear the harmony. I felt the peculiar elation of being in a city where no one knew me, and I could explore the possibilities for perversion without encumbrance. I drank pints of bitters in corner pubs and wrote in my journal. I visited a prostitute, but could not get an erection. She sat me on the edge of the bed in her basement flat and efficiently jerked me off with a vibrator.

But I was not completely sunk. The fishy depths of degradation rejected me. I bobbed towards the surface and found myself, one day, sitting on the pavement with a crowd of chanting protesters in front of the gray stone facade of the South African Embassy. Pigeons wheeled in the air above us and watched impassively from the statute of Lord Nelson in Trafalgar Square as we shouted our condemnation of the massacre of Blacks in the South African township of Sharpville. The grieving, terror-stricken faces of peaceful black demonstrators running from a hail of dum dum bullets and carrying the dying bodies of their brothers and sisters had greeted us from the front pages of the morning paper. We had marched from the University in hasty protest, and when the police arrived, we sat and refused to move. We were promptly arrested without incident, loaded into black police lorries, and carted off to jail, from which we were soon released due to the intervention of a member of parliament.

Soon after my arrest, I met Prudence, who was a fellow student at the London School of Economics. She was studying statistics. We went out a few times, and decided to try living together. We found a basement apartment off Portabello Road. It was sparsely furnished, but it had a bed that was ours, and we would lie in it together and make love. In the midst of our lovemaking I told myself that I did not really love her, that she was somewhat ordinary in appearance with her round face, glasses, and straight brown hair; but after all I was no great catch, and I liked playing house with her. The sounds of the street floated in through our window. Side-by-side, we purchased provisions at an outdoor market two blocks away. Old men peered nearsightedly at the produce, mothers with children in tow shouted reprimands as they searched in their purses for change, and couples like ourselves strolled from stall to stall with their arms around each other. The market was always loud and rowdy with life. We would return, resupplied, to our basement lair, cook, wash dishes, read the newspaper, and go to bed. It felt finally as if I had crossed that magical threshold that separates children from adults. Prudence was not a masturbatory fantasy. She was a real flesh and blood woman. And playing house with her, I was becoming a little more real, a little more flesh and blood, instead of a gray cloud of thought above and an urge below that twanged unceremoniously whenever it would.

A few months before I was to return to the United States, Prudence discovered she was pregnant. She cried. I was not ready for a child. Neither, really was she. She agreed to have an abortion. Getting one was not so easy. Abortion was still illegal. We rode on red buses to secret appointments with a kindly Jamaican doctor who performed the operation. There were no complications. Prudence recuperated in our bed. She was sad. She said she wanted to come back to the United States with me. I could not imagine it. We took a last trip together through the Netherlands and I flew back home without her.

I returned to Swarthmore for an uneventful senior year, during which I shared my alienation with a small circle of friends, who rivaled each other in ostentatious displays of disaffection.

Mine was the last apolitical class at Swarthmore, the last to wallow in its alienation. In 1962, the year after I graduated, Students for a Democratic Society (SDS), the most important organization of radical students to emerge during the Sixties, held its founding convention in Ann Arbor. Later that same year, the first Swarthmore SDS chapter was founded. The student movement transformed campus life. The tranquil botanical garden became a hotbed of agitation. Eight years after I graduated, African-American students occupied the admissions office to demand changes in admission policies and the creation of a Black Cultural Center. Seven days later, Courtney Smith, the president of the college, collapsed and died of a heart attack. The *New York Times* blamed his death on the Black students.[5]

The waves of protest, pounding the shores of academia with such force, hit just as I stepped off the beach. I didn't even get my feet wet. It was time to graduate. I felt condemned to be a college professor like my fathers before me. I didn't even consider another path. Seeing no alternative, I enrolled in the graduate history program at Yale.

Yale was an arrogant gray fortress in the center of a sullen resentful working class town. I rented an attic room within biking distance of the campus. I still felt like the underground man, perverse and obsessive. Why was I studying the peculiarities of Reformation theology? In my attic apartment I'd sit in front of my typewriter, unable to write three sentences. I'd doodle and stare out the window for hours, then undress, stick a finger up my ass, and masturbate. I fantasized about women stripping me naked and beating me on the ass.

I spent more time masturbating and doodling than studying. My doodles turned into elaborate drawings. I hung them on the walls of my apartment. When spring came I trudged to the library like a man returning to prison. Along the way I passed art students, stretched out on the lawn, sketching trees, buildings, and each other. Their bodies pressed lazily into the grass. My body carried my mind like a porter bearing luggage. My flesh was a diseased appendage of a corrupted mind. Their flesh was a doorway through which the world entered.

Among the art students was a woman I knew from Swarthmore. She had a boyfriend, a hearty Greek who painted large juicy oil paintings of raw meat. I finally worked up the courage to invite them over to look at my drawings. They complimented me, told me my work was as good as any art student's, and urged me to continue.

I had first begun to draw under the tutelage of my aunt Susan. She lived alone in a lovely little two-room apartment on the top floor of an old brick town house in Greenwich Village. Susan worked in the garment industry, expediting the shipment of shirts from factory to outlet. Deeply lonely and constantly annoyed by the pettiness of her fellow workers, she lavished affection on me, and quietly sought to instill in me her love of art. She took me on painting expeditions to the sites of abandoned factories and rusting railroad tracks where we would set up our little easels and paint for a few hours till I got cold or hungry. She let me leaf through her voluminous collection of art books and took me to the Metropolitan Museum where her favorites were the El Grecos.

I had never thought of our painting expeditions as anything

but a pleasant diversion, an escape from the rigorous discipline required to master the intricacies of ideas. I was born to the craft of intellectual production. I had to keep my hands clean. And yet I loved to smear the colors on my palette, to dab them on my brush and mark, in what felt like almost perfect freedom, the white surface of the canvas boards on which we painted. Art was silent. It did not participate in arguments. But its silence was not the silence of a student who does not know the answer. Art was not tongue-tied. In the making of art, the material world almost rose to the dignity of the disembodied world of concepts.

At the end of my first year at Yale, I told my mother that I intended to drop out, move to the Lower East Side of New York, and become a painter. She asked me a few practical questions—where was I going to live, how was I going to make a living—and accepted my perfunctory answers without argument. I was making a foolish choice. What could she do? She was happy now with Herbert. I could go on with my life. She would go on with hers. My failure to row towards some professorial safe harbor was no longer her responsibility. My boat was drifting rudderless towards dangerous turbulence. It was not the heroic example of the civil rights movement in the South that led me to drop out of college. It was the insistent pressure of private misery.

I could be a painter!

THE LOWER EAST SIDE

In the Sixties, the Lower East Side was a predominantly Puerto Rican ghetto. Floating in the broad stream of Puerto Rican life were remnants of previous immigrant migrations. The Jews, who had worked in the shirt factories and cigar manufacturing establishments on Cooper Union Square, had mostly moved on to better things, leaving behind a few good delicatessens. Old Ukrainians dozed on the benches of Tompkins Square Park, spat occasionally into the dirt, and worried about the neighborhood. At the Odessa Restaurant on Avenue A, they ate beet soup with two slices of dark bread for 35 cents, next to poets, jazz musicians, and painters driven from Greenwich Village by rising rents.

For me, the Lower East Side was the anti-suburb, the polar opposite of Riverdale, Newton, and Swarthmore. People here could not afford the manicured distances favored by the middle class. They brushed up against each other, breathed in each other's faces, and woke each other up at night playing the radio too loud or fighting with the window open. The streets were all stains and clutter. They smelled of piss, mildew, roach powder, and rotting garbage. Refuse and filth blanketed the empty lots. Weeds sprouted between middens of mattress springs, rusting car parts, old clothes and beer cans. Nothing was new, nothing clean, nothing reflected pride of possession. The floors in the railroad apartments groaned beneath layers of cheap linoleum. The ceilings were heavy with peeling paint. Roaches overran kitchens. You could hear the rats scurrying at night in the walls. Everything material threatened to collapse into gray anonymous wretchedness. But life continued like a fever in a failing body.

In the midst of it all, Tompkins Square Park was a leafy refuge. On the east side was a little playground where women watched toddlers clambering onto swings and sliding down the slide into the dirt. At the south end was an empty bandstand. Throughout the remainder of the park, circular paths wound between iron fences, behind which the grass grew like an exotic animal, caged in for its own protection. In the 1850s, '60s, and '70s the park had been the scene of many demonstrations. On January 13, 1874, thousands of unemployed workers who had rallied here to demand government relief were beaten out of the park by a mob of club wielding mounted police. Now the iron fences prevented large assemblies, and at least for the time being tranquility prevailed.

My first Lower East Side apartment was a railroad flat on 7th Street between Avenues C and D. A row of four rooms ran from the front to the back of the building. Only the rooms at either end had windows. Holes cut in the interior walls let a little light into the ones in the middle. In typical Lower East Side fashion, the bathtub was in the kitchen. It had a metal cover so it could double as a dinner table.

I set up my easel in the kitchen and began to paint. Empty tubes of acrylic piled up next to dishes crusted with old spaghetti sauce. Roaches ran across my pallet. Paint smeared on my sheets, on the doorknobs, on the phone receiver, on the faucets in the sink. Canvases hung in every available space, and leaned up against each other in the corners. I began a meticulous study of the plumbing. Over and over again I painted the bathtub with its baked enamel cover. I painted the kitchen sink. I painted the porcelain bowl of the toilet peeking out from the open door of its closet. I would spend hours carefully studying the perspective of these objects, exploring the relation between lines vanishing in space and lines converging in two dimensions on a canvas. I was fascinated by the tension between surface design and illusion of depth. The laws of perspective were neat and clean. They imposed an implacable order on the chaos of visual experience. They tamed the savage beast of sensation. In my paintings there was never any clutter, no dirty dishes, no soiled socks, no trash on the floor, no stains on the linoleum. I painted serene interiors in ironic homage to my obsession with dirt and excrement.

Like a child playing dress up who tries on the grownup's clothing and examines the effect in the mirror, I tried on the role of artist, and checked for signs that it suited me. I knew the odds were not good. Setting out to be an artist was like setting out to win the lottery. But what fun! Playing in the brightly colored mud, I lost and found myself. I curved with the curve of the sink. I aligned myself with the edge of the bathtub. Out of disorder and untrammeled possibility, an order grew on the canvas and in my life. Out of the perfect freedom emerged necessity, not imposed from outside, not stifling and repressive, not the antithesis of freedom, but its fulfillment.

I enrolled in the Brooklyn Museum School of Fine Arts. Twice a week, I dutifully drew a still life of bottles, balls, cylinders, and cubes, which the teacher arranged at the beginning of the class on a stand in the center of the room. We ringed the still life with our easels like a besieging army and tried to "capture" it on our newsprint pads. The teacher walked behind us commenting on our degrees of success. It never surrendered. It was always there at the end of class. Mocking us. And boring. I soon lost interest in the exercise and managed to get myself expelled for being disruptive.

I continued to paint my toilet bowl, my sink, and my beloved bathtub. When I finished one painting, I would move my easel a few feet to the left or right and begin another. The change altered the vanishing point of the perspective and transformed the geometry of the composition. Shadows and colors varied with the weather and the time of day. The material provided by my cramped kitchen seemed inexhaustible. But as bathtub succeeded bathtub, I experienced a growing fear. What if I abandoned my self-imposed limitations? Why bathtubs and sinks? Why not bedrooms and chairs? Or rooftops and chimneys? The choice was completely arbitrary, as was the choice to represent anything at all. Why bother to get the perspective right? Why not pure abstraction? I had no answers. All I knew was that within my narrow framework I could achieve a semblance of order. Outside it, the floodgates of chaotic expression could swallow me. There would be no reason to put a line one place rather than another, no boundaries, no limits. The shit would hit the fan.

In the middle of my bathtub period, I got a part time job writing capsule reviews for *Art News Magazine*. The galleries I visited were inevitably empty, presided over by condescending, poorly paid attendants who made a point of looking bored as I walked around jotting down my notes. I quickly learned I was not alone in building my art on arbitrary foundations. There was not much rhyme or reason in what I saw. Artists strove for an identifiable trademark. Frank Stella did flat paintings of nesting rectangles; Roy Lichtenstein, enlarged cartoon images; Jasper Johns, scumbled, texturized American flags and maps.

The only unpardonable sin was to be out of fashion, to be caught wearing the styles of the last century, the last year, the last month. Better to go naked. No one dared say that the avant-garde emperor had no clothes. Too much money was at stake. If you refused to accept the avant-garde on its own terms, you were stuck in the past and suspected of harboring a secret passion for Norman Rockwell's *Saturday Evening Post* covers.

As I became increasingly disillusioned with the art I found in the uptown galleries, I could not help but question the arbitrary constraints I imposed on my own work. Almost overnight, I lost the compulsion to paint plumbing and abandoned my bathtub series. The problems I had been struggling with no longer mattered. I took to constructing huge grotesque collages of scabrous junk scavenged on nighttime strolls through the Lower East Side: pee-stained mattresses, discarded women's undergarments, old shoes, cigarette butts, broken dolls, all glued together with melted wax. They covered entire walls of my apartment. It was as if all the plumbing of my bathtub series had backed up, and overflowed. A friend who hung one of my smaller works over his bed was horrified one evening to find an army of cockroaches crawling down towards his pillow from their hiding place in an old boot I'd retrieved from the garbage on one of my excursions.

My last bathtub painting was the only one in which some of the characteristic clutter of my apartment made a cameo appearance: The plumbing appeared in flaming reds and greens. Beneath the bathtub was the boot that later provided shelter to the cockroaches. Next to it was a photograph torn from the newspaper. It showed the nearly naked corpse of a Vietnamese peasant dragged by a rope behind an American troop carrier. An American soldier looked back casually as if checking to see that the trailer was still properly hitched to the pick up. It was 1966. The war was in full swing. The Sixties was more than half over. I had yet to take the plunge into its boisterous rapids, a baptism that in due course would make the solitary preoccupations of the artist seem a curious anachronism.

For Me, the Lower East Side Was the Anti-suburb.

TAKING THE PLUNGE

My arrival on the Lower East Side coincided with that of a new wave of immigrants. They were mostly white, long-haired, dropouts who at first had no collective name for themselves. The media, when it woke up to their existence, called them "hippies." They set up crash pads in rundown tenements, dragged their mattresses onto the floor, and formed fragile, ever changing communities. They sent many hours hanging out on St. Marks Place, panhandling in front of Gem's Spa, and getting stoned on the benches of Tompkins Square Park.

They were like confetti blown from a party in some other part of town onto the Puerto Rican streets of the ghetto. By and large they were oblivious to their neighbors. They stayed because the rents were cheap and the Lower East Side didn't seem to belong to anybody. They could do more or less what they wanted and dress as they pleased. No one was going to tell them to get a job. Their migration reversed the route of their predecessors. To prior generations of immigrants the Lower East Side had been the gateway to America. For the dropouts of the Sixties, it was an exit door. They came to the ghetto fleeing America, not trying to gain entrance. They were escaping from the emotional dust bowl of their families, their schools, their jobs. Stoned at night, they would stare in the windows of the corner bodega, watch the mice scurrying over piles of green plantains and sweet potatoes, and breathe a sigh of relief. Home was far away.

Most of them were younger than I, but they had a lot to teach me. They brought the political counterculture of the Sixties to my doorstep. They were an infectious ferment spreading through the bowels of the ghetto. They agitated the intricate privacy of my apartment, which was now full to overflowing with enormous assemblages of Lower East Side garbage.

I began writing an extended essay about the end of avant-garde art. I wrote that painting was lost in a meaningless play with limits that no one cared about any longer. The libratory promise of art was now to be achieved outside the frame of the canvas by the total imaginative transformation of reality.

I typed away in my apartment, setting the typewriter on the lid of the bathtub, but never finished. I was like a nervous swimmer arguing myself into jumping from a high rock into the river. Once I jumped there was no reason to continue the argument.

Somewhere, a dam had broken. The miasma of alienation that had enveloped a generation condensed into a great flood of disaffection. The rising waters swept the hippies out of their homes and into the ghetto. It threatened to tear the rotting clapboard of public and private life from its foundations. It seemed only a matter of time before the tide would reach everywhere. There was no escaping, and on my part, no desire to escape.

What broke the dam? Too many rotting corpses dragged through the rice fields of Vietnam? Too many Black children beaten on the evening news. Who knows? We who are in the business of undermining dams don't really know what makes them go. We're always taken by surprise when they do.

In order to stay afloat in the flood it was necessary to discard some baggage. All the accoutrements with which we protected our privacy had to go. It was like a baptism. We immersed ourselves in the water and emerged as members of a new tribe. We left the old behind. We would have new friends, new relations, a new family. The Vietnamese peasant harvesting rice with a rifle on her shoulder, the civil rights worker registering voters in Mississippi—they were our brothers and sisters. We would share with them the danger and the victory. I had missed the first half of the Sixties. SNCC had been founded in 1960, the year of the first sit-ins. In 1961 Black and White Freedom Riders sitting together on Greyhound buses drove into Birmingham Alabama and were beaten with pipes and chains by a Ku Klux Klan–led mob. In 1963 Vietnamese Buddhist monks turned themselves into flaming torches to protest the war. President Johnson began bombing North Vietnam in 1965. It was now the waning months of 1966. Earlier in the year James Meredith had been shot in Mississippi. Buddhist monks were again setting themselves on fire in Vietnam.

And I was preparing to make up for lost time.

* * *

My plunge into the countercultural politics of the Lower East Side began in January 1967 when I noticed fliers posted around the streets calling for artists to participate in an Angry Arts week to protest the war in Vietnam. I started going to organizing meetings. The artists who attended the meetings on the Lower East Side were an oddly assorted mix of actors in street theater groups, stray poets, and painters. Michael Brown was there from the Pageant Players, and so was Peter Schumann from the Bread and Puppet theater. And there was Ben Morea, an anarchist painter.

We met in crowded apartments. Some of us squatted on the

bare floor while others of us sat on brokeback sofas and leaned against the walls. We smoked and talked about the need for art to be a tool of the struggle. As artists, we had an obligation to use our skills in support of the movement. Our angry art had a purpose—to encourage people to oppose the war in Vietnam. The orthodoxy espoused by the avant-garde establishment held that true art doesn't have a purpose. Art is for art's sake. Propaganda and pornography, tools to arouse the masses on the one hand and the genitals on the other, were excluded from the temple of true art and confined to squat outbuildings on its outskirts. We could care less.

The avant-garde artists sipping cocktails in the living rooms of wealthy patrons, and guzzling wine at 57th Street gallery openings, were irrelevant. They played at revolutionary intent while cultivating marketable outrages. We were the real thing. We had little time to waste on subtle theoretical discussions of aesthetics. There were demonstrations to organize, leaflets to produce.

I listened to the organizers express their opinions. I compared myself to them. They all seemed very strong, certain of themselves, formed. There were no famous artists in the room. But famous artists had bought their fame at too heavy a price. Here was something potentially better, membership in a group with a handle on history.

* * *

I threw myself into Angry Arts week with enthusiasm. Here was a way out of isolation and introversion, a way to flush the residue of guilty sexuality with a fresh stream of legitimate shared anger. The photographs of napalmed children and burning villages pouring out of Vietnam had not made me angry. Somewhere in my childhood I had lost my ability to feel angry. But they were a call to step outside the closed universe of my subjectivity, to stand with others, to push in the real world against the horror. And perhaps, standing there with others, anger would come to me as a blessing, as a release.

For me art had always been a place of peace. It was something I did quietly by myself. I'm not sure now, and wondered even then, if art can ever be truly angry, no matter how angry the artist who produces it. Art stands against and reconciles with horror. It can make horror beautiful. But I was prepared to waive my intellectual reservations. I was done with thought that interfered with action. If art could not join in the struggle, I was prepared to jettison the art.*

* * *

In early adolescence I had discovered a book of Goya's etchings in a bookcase in our living room. I would sneak the volume down from its shelf, take it up to my room, close the door, and leaf through the unflinching depictions of murder and sexual violence. Bodies of slaughtered prisoners lay heaped in tangled piles like garbage. A firing squad executed blindfolded prisoners tied to stakes. Women were raped and women begged not to be raped. Naked corpses without arms or legs hung on trees like meat in a butcher shop. In one etching two soldiers held a naked prisoner upside down with his legs apart so a third could split him down the middle with a sword. In another a mob exacted revenge on a soldier who was being dragged along the ground by a rope tied to his legs. He had been stripped of his pants and a man shoved a stake

---

*Abbie Hoffman was less inclined to put aside his reservations. "Demanding that artists do antiwar art is like demanding that chefs cook antiwar food," he wrote in a letter to the *Village Voice*, in which he criticized the whole concept of an Angry Arts Week, arguing that artists should "transcend anger" in their work and affirm life (from *For the Hell of It: The Life and Times of Abbie Hoffman*, Jonah Raskin California: 1996, p. 84).

into his anus. The captions beneath the pictures were terse: "What Madness," "A Cruel Shame," "Forced to Look." They neither explained nor consoled.

I remember in particular an etching of a child being spanked. The child has broken a pitcher, which can be seen in the background. His punishment is being administered by an old woman who pins him across her knees with her left hand. She holds his skirts up in her teeth revealing his buttocks. In her right hand she holds a shoe with which she beats him. I masturbated to this image. Goya was a great artist. His work was part of my cultural heritage. It did not need to be hidden, like the tattered black and white photograph of a chained naked woman that I picked up on the street one evening and secreted in a hole in the bottom of a bookshelf in my room. But Goya was my first pornographer.

Sitting in my Lower East Side flat after our meetings, I thought about Goya. He went deaf and mad. The title plate of his *Caprichios* bares the caption: "The dream of reason brings forth monsters." I imagined him hunched over his etching plate, gouging into it by candle light, gouging, gouging deep into the night. He clenches his etching burin until his hand aches. Spread out on his work table are all the reassuring solid materials of his art—his acids, engraving tools and copper plates. He digs his burin into the plate. As he draws the groove of the buttocks his burin pushes into it. Who is he at that moment? The child who is being beaten or the woman who beats him? Is he the penis of the rapist or the vagina of the raped? Is he the sword of the dismemberer or the body of the dismembered? Is he the gray sky above the man hanging from the gallows or his dead unseeing eyes? Is he all of these or none of them? Whose side was Goya on? Was he angry when he drew, or lost in a more complex mood?

SACRILEGE

On Monday, January 23, 1967, the *New York Times* reported on a demonstration organized by the Lower East Side contingent of Angry Arts week:

> Twenty-three peace demonstrators unfurled posters portraying a maimed Vietnamese child in the central aisle of St. Patrick's Cathedral during the ten o'clock high mass yesterday morning, causing the celebrant to interrupt the liturgy. . . In a statement they left with a friend, the protesters said they were leaving the church in the midst of the ceremony "out of disrespect for Cardinal Spellman" to protest his recent statement that "the war in Vietnam is a war for civilization." The paper posters carried the fifth of the Ten Commandments, "Thou shall not kill" above the child's photograph and below it the legend, "Vietnam." They were no sooner unfurled than the demonstrators were surrounded by detectives and plain-clothes patrolmen who had been tipped off that a demonstration would take place.

The *Times*, at least in this instance, was a model of journalistic accuracy. No sooner had I stood up and begun to extract the rolled cardboard from under my tweed overcoat, than I was surrounded by burly men in black trench coats. I was passed from one of them to the other out into the vestibule, where I was I.D.'d and informed I was being charged with disorderly conduct, unlawful assembly in a church, and disruption of a religious ceremony. In the firm grip of my arresting officer, I was escorted out of the dark church into bright winter sunlight. As I was loaded into the paddy wagon I managed to catch a glimpse of photographers, a picket line, and a crowd of onlookers standing in on the sidewalk. The door slammed shut and the van drove off, carrying my fellow arrestees and me first to the local precinct and then to a holding cell at the Central Police Station, 100 Center Street, affectionately known as "the Tombs."

We spent the night in jail. A jailor brought us pineapple marmalade sandwiches and cocoa. We talked quietly among ourselves and then someone began chanting "Hare Krishna, Hare Krishna, Hare Rama Hare Rama." We all joined in, and as we chanted I relaxed, the tension flowed out of me, and I began to feel an enormous peace, as if a tense journey that had consumed my entire life was coming to an end. I had arrived at my destination.

I chanted quietly along with the rest of my cellmates. And as I chanted, all at once, it seemed that the harsh light in the cell—glaring on the naked walls, reflecting off the stainless steel toilet—underwent a transformation, becoming simultaneously brighter, clearer, and softer. There I was, having a "mystical experience." I felt a twinge of disloyalty to the rationality I had learned to admire while listening to the dinner table conversation of my parents. But those days seemed far away. There was no need to feel ashamed in any case. Such experiences were a sign of the times. The membranes separating various compartments of the counterculture were permeable. Their contents flowed together. Just let yourself go, the times were whispering, and you'll be saved.

We were bailed out the next day. I returned, reluctantly, to the solitude of my railroad flat with its familiar mess, canvases stacked against the wall, and roaches feeding in the garbage. I set my typewriter on the enamel cover of the bathtub next to the sink in my kitchen, pushed away the dishes, and poured out a pornographic fantasy in which Cardinal Spellman is sexually humiliated in front of his congregation, choir boys are sodomized, and his congregation stripped and beaten. Pausing to catch my breath, I continued:

> . . . One must be just in one's fantasies. One must not allow oneself to be lenient. Difficult as it may be one must force oneself to imagine ever new indecencies to inflict on criminals who are the embodiment of real obscenity. Only in one's fantasies can one preserve for future generations the image of justice that perhaps it will be their joy to inflict. It is an obligation which one must fulfill in private.

> Nothing inhibits the carrying out of this obligation more drastically than this action. To give way to the temptation to turn one's fantasies into reality is an unmitigated disaster. For immediately one is lost in a world in which they, the obscene ones rule. Their laws apply, their game is played, their dance is danced. Everything one says is used against one: one must become sincere, witness one's ethical convictions, proclaim oneself willing to suffer for those convictions, make sacrifices.

> . . . Beware of action! Beware of its temptations! Preserve the truth inside you! Publish it privately among your friends. Live by it secretly. Draw strength from it. Reveal it to broader circles only in veiled allegories. But do not act on it. Do not witness it. Deny it under oath.

And if the desire to act is too strong, do something half-hearted. Picket outside the Cathedral. Run the peace candidate. Proclaim the possibility and necessity of moral outrage (do not admit that you have passed beyond outrage to something harder, glittering, vicious) Do not show your teeth. Be very careful. Shake hands with the right people. Smile. But inside, keep the faith. . . .

Ethics is a bog. They have made it an instrument against us. They have poisoned its waters. It is the most tempting part of their system and the most dangerous. In defense one must become inhuman. One must cling to one's inhumanity, spit full in the face of their poisoned platitudes so that beyond those platitudes, beyond our own inhumanity there is preserved the possibility of a true ethics that will exist not in the minds of the moralist, but in our mutual happiness.

A-men
Fuck off!

The outrages I perpetrated in my imagination far outdistanced the mild disturbance we had created in reality.

Our disruption of Cardinal Spellman's mass—a moral act, committed in the name of napalmed babies whose pain and suffering we asked the world to witness—had another dimension. It was an intrusion, a rending of the veil of civility, an invasion of the rabble into the sanctimonious safe house of the hypocrites.

It was not extraordinary that I, in the seclusion of my apartment, wrote "unacceptable" reflections in my journal. It was extraordinary how quickly, and with how little mediation, these private fantasies would enter the arena of public political discourse. In the mimeographed fliers I produced for the Motherfuckers, they emerged almost verbatim. Private fantasy freed itself to roam the streets, titillating the police who picked my ravings out of the gutter and preserved them in their files as evidence of the terrible menace we represented.

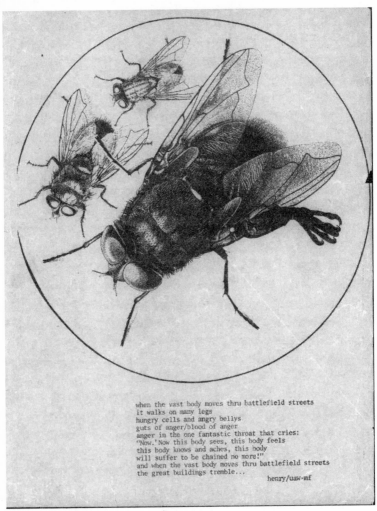

when the vast body moves thru battlefield streets
it walks on many legs
hungry cells and angry bellys
guts of anger/blood of anger
anger in the one fantastic throat that cries:
"Now.'Now this body sees, this body feels
this body knows and aches, this body
will suffer to be chained no more!"
and when the vast body moves thru battlefield streets
the great buildings tremble...
       henry/uaw-mf

A poem by Rex Weiner we put out as a flier.

BEN MOREA AND THE FOUNDING OF THE MOTHERFUCKERS

When Angry Arts week ended, a group of Lower East side artists continued to meet with the intention of carrying on where Angry Arts week had left off. We eventually decided to call ourselves "the Motherfuckers," short for "Up Against the Wall Motherfucker." The name came from a line in Leroi Jones's prose poem "Black People!" that he'd written as his hometown, Newark, was erupting in a riot sparked by police brutality:

> . . . you can't steal nothin from a white man, he's already stole it he owes you anything you want, even his life. All the stores will open if you will say the magic words. The magic words are: Up against the wall mother fucker this is a stick up![6]

Our name had the advantage that it could not be spoken in polite company. That which could not be spoken, could not be co-opted.

The unacknowledged leader of our group was Ben Morea. His life story could not have been more different from my own. He had grown up in Hell's Kitchen on the West Side of Manhattan and lived all his life on the streets of New York. He never knew his father. He loved jazz and learned to play the vibes. He hung out in clubs where heroin was hip and got hooked. That period of his life ended after he was busted for possession. He kicked his heroin habit cold turkey in prison, but in the process became so sick that he almost died. He was transferred from his cell to the prison ward of a hospital. There, in the art therapy room, he did his first paintings.

Ben had tried to kick his habit many times, but always he would go back to the jazz scene and get hooked again. When he left the hospital, he decided he was done. He put away his vibes, stopped going to the clubs, and started painting. While looking to fill the void in his life left when he abandoned the jazz world, he met Judith Malina and Julian Beck, the founders of the Living Theater, an improvisational anarcho-pacifist theater of communal ritual and provocation. Judith and Julian were Ben's introduction to anarchism. After meeting them he joined a study group organized by Murray Bookchin. It met in Murray's apartment on 9th Street east of 1st Avenue. Murray was a pugnacious working class intellectual, committed to anarchism and interested in technology and ecology. Ben was never entirely comfortable with the intellectual theorizing that went on in the group. According to Murray, he would show up, listen impatiently for a while, and then start screaming. He'd call everybody a petty bourgeois white honky and storm out. Everyone thought that was the last they'd see of him, but the next meeting he would be back, and go through the same ritual. Even after the group disbanded, Ben would show up regularly at Murray's home to talk and argue politics.

Ben began searching for a way to turn art into an instrument of revolution, which meant to turn art against itself. He wanted to destroy art in the name of art—and life. With Roy Hahne he put out *Black Mask*, a four-page magazine in which he published his manifestos. Ben gathered together a group of likeminded artists. They called themselves Black Mask after the magazine and proceeded to stage a series of theatrical provocations.

On October 10, 1966, they traveled uptown from the Lower East Side, with the intention of shutting down the Museum of Modern Art. They had handed out fliers announcing their action in advance. At the entrance to the museum they were met by barricades and a line of cops. Art, which refused engagement, now required police protection. It was a victory.

On another occasion they announced they would change the name of Wall Street to "War Street." Ben and his fellow provocateurs concealed their faces behind black woolen ski masks and paraded down the street carrying skull masks on stakes while handing out fliers proclaiming the name change.

A January 1968 action targeted the poet and playwright Kenneth Koch. Koch was a friend of abstract expressionists and a beloved professor of poetry at Columbia University. His poems were often playful, endearing, and somewhat obscure, but never "political" or angry. He did not write to put anyone up against the wall. Ben learned that he was scheduled to give a reading at St. Mark's Church on the Lower East Side. Newark was erupting in riots, and Leroi Jones had just been arrested for carrying firearms and resisting arrest. Black Maskers made a flier with a picture of Jones, shackled and chained, his arms behind his back. He had what looked like a bloody welt on his forehead. Below the picture were three words: "Poetry is Revolution." Ben and his cohorts took seats in the balcony. One member of the group, a man over six feet tall with a great head of tousled black hair, wore a trench coat. He looked impressively sinister, the very image of a turn-of-the-century anarchist bomb thrower. Concealed under his coat was a pistol. As Koch began to read, the man stood up. He shouted, "Koch!" When the poet looked up, the man aimed the pistol and fired. It was loaded with blanks. There was a loud explosion, and according to Ben, Koch fainted on the spot.* Ben and his cohorts threw their fliers from the balcony and ran out of the church.

Ben was short, wiry, and intense. He spoke in little thrusts and jabs that mirrored his physical mannerisms. His walk had a slight swagger and he had a way of cocking his head to one side and hitching himself up when preparing for a confrontation that might have seemed ridiculous in someone else.

But Ben was not ridiculous. Ben's strength lay in the fact that, in a non-trivial sense, he was true to his word. A lot of words flew around recklessly in the Sixties, but the gap between rhetoric and reality seemed smaller with him than with anybody else I knew at the time. He did what he said he would do. This was his code of honor, the code of the street, to which he adhered with the discipline of a martial artist. He was calm and focused in battle, able to calibrate his actions in moments of tension, while all around him, less hardened street fighters like me panicked and struggled not to flee from danger. In those moments of confrontation, with the police charging down on us, I was acutely aware of the limits of my courage. The little bird of my being, silent, private, separate, would become frantic to protect itself. I could no more force myself to take risks than a drowning man could keep from struggling for breath.

At the time I thought of Ben as possessing street intelligence that was the equivalent and polar opposite of Herbert's book intelligence. Ben's code of honor challenged all the training of my childhood in the relation of word to deed. As a child, lis-

* An unsourced entry on Koch in Wikipedia has a less dramatic description of what happened and says nothing about his fainting: "The poet regained his composure and said to the "shooter," "Grow up."

tening to the grownups talk, I concluded that thought must be isolated from action. My fathers' minds floated from thought to thought in a thought-world separate from the world of doing and making. Ben's thought flowed naturally and directly into action. Before joining the Motherfuckers, I had lived isolated in a whirl of words and guilty fantasies. My encounter with Ben hurled me from my isolation with awful suddenness. I felt I could only imitate, posture, make tentative steps to follow where he led, and hope that no one would notice my cowardice, my fear, my innocence.

Very quickly, or so it seems to me now, the Motherfuckers was transformed under Ben's leadership from a group which met to plan activities into something quite different—an identity. Involvement stopped being a matter of merely attending meetings. It became a question of "being" a Motherfucker. We lived to throw ourselves into the fray. We gave up attachments to the past. We abandoned our family names in favor of "Motherfucker." Tom Neumann died and Tom Motherfucker was born.

* * *

At the core of the Motherfuckers were ten to fifteen fully committed regulars around whom gathered a group of fellow travelers whose commitment varied, and who preferred to keep some level of safe distance. College students were drawn to us by the possibility of living the total revolution. Drop out kids hanging on the street found in us a family of fellow seekers, slightly older than themselves, to substitute for the one they left behind. We were adopted by a group of Puerto Rican street kids. They came to our events, ate at our community feasts, and hung out in our crash pads. The winos with whom we shared the streets organized themselves into the "Wine Group for Freedom" a.k.a. "The Wine Nation." Ben folded them under our wing. Except for our core group, it was never entirely clear who was and was not a Motherfucker. We didn't have membership cards. If you spent enough time with us, and you wished to be a Motherfucker, and participated in our actions, you became part of the family.

The vicissitudes of male emotional life dominated the Motherfuckers. Women played a distinctly ancillary role in all matters. Their most acceptable role was to be someone's girlfriend or "old lady." If the relationship ended, they tended to drift away. They did the traditional women's work of cooking for the group, helping to prepare the community feasts we organized, nursing babies, and tending to the bruised egos of the men. But they also hawked our fliers, got arrested (rarely) at our demonstrations, yelled at the cops, and stole credit cards to finance various nefarious adventures. Once, when Deputy Inspector Fink, the commander of the Lower East Side's Ninth Precinct, was scheduled to speak at a community meeting, they organized their own women's demonstration. They dressed up in their most colorful skirts and scarves and jangly jewelry. Carole Motherfucker strapped her baby Chacha to her back and when Fink's turn came to speak they swirled, hooting and hollering, down the aisles of Cooper Union, and drove him off the stage.

No matter how often women took part in our activities, they rarely participated in our long tense political arguments. Among the men this was expected, acceptable and went without comment. Occasionally women would demand attention, raise their voice and challenge the men. Some were more outspoken than others. But political argument was men's work. As our arguments went on, hour after hour, the stakes would gradually rise to the point where the issue was no longer a disagreement about strategy or tactics, but about our strength of character and commitment. Ben was always vigilant in his search for weakness, and insistent in his demands for loyalty. The commitment he demanded, and that we were quick to demand of each other, knew no boundaries. We concealed our vulnerability. Ben rewarded us with the promise to protect us with his life. He would be withering about our weaknesses and taunt us for our timidity. But when we did well in his eyes, he would reward us with a look of intense affection that became the most valued currency of the group.

We knew each other through the daily life we shared. We did not engage in long conversations about where we came from and how we got to where we were. We shed our anchors to the past in private. The Marines take in new recruits and systematically strip them of the traces of their former identities. They are given crew cuts and handed a uniform. The Motherfuckers took in recruits for a quite different army, a long-haired army of urban guerillas. The new identities we adopted did not, of course, obliterate the old. Little as we cared to dwell on our differences, the mix of self-doubt and assurance with which we entered into our new life depended in part on whether we were men or women, middle class or working class, college educated or not, in our teens or twenties. It mattered whether we were raised in the country or the city, and whether we were white—almost all of us were, at least in the core group—or a person of color. It's hard to find a common thread in our various backgrounds or in the paths that led us to the Motherfuckers. We were like the cast of characters in a Hollywood disaster movie, thrown together by circumstances, forced to depend upon each other, and bringing to our predicament a range of strengths and weaknesses.

The disaster that threw us together was America. We left homes, jobs, high schools and colleges driven by a diversity of dissatisfactions. Vietnam was a big part of the problem. The war was immoral, pointless, and obscene. Each invitation to come to our local draft board for a physical was a stepping-stone into a gaping maw that would chew us up and turn us into bloody chowder. But Vietnam, awful as it might be, was only a symptom of a larger problem. We were repelled by the world our parents had learned to accept. And we were attracted by the promise of a better world awaiting.

For those of us who grew up with parents who espoused some form of radical politics, becoming a Motherfucker was our way to strike out on our own path, and re-imagine a revolutionary tradition. For others whose parents were Goldwater Republicans, the Motherfuckers was a parallel universe. But in all cases the choice to join the Motherfuckers was a rejection of our families of origin. No one joined the Motherfuckers with the blessing of their parents, be they Goldwater Republicans or card-carrying Communists.

What were we? A political organization? A commune? Ben used the term "affinity group," a translation of "*groupa affinidad*" used by Spanish anarchists to describe the cellular structures of their underground movement. He was introduced to the term in discussions with Murray Bookchin. In a manifesto printed in the form of a flier, Ben wrote:

> The affinity group is the seed/term/essence of organization. It is coming together out of mutual Need or Desire: cohesive historical groups unite out of the shared necessities of the struggle for survival, while dreaming of the possibility of love.
>
> In the pre-revolutionary period affinity groups must assemble to project a revolutionary consciousness to develop forms for particular struggles. In the revolutionary period itself they will emerge as armed cadres

at the centers of conflict, and in the post-revolution-
ary period suggest forms for the new everyday life.

Some people described us as a "street gang with an analysis." In retrospect, I think we had some of the characteristics
of a cult. But for Ben—the Italian street kid who grew up, as
he says, "pretty much on his own"; who did not know his
father; who, even when he was sitting in jail in Boston and
facing twenty-five years for stabbing a man, did not want to
tell his mother he was a Motherfucker because he did not
want to disappoint her—we were first and foremost, and
remain to this day, "the family." *Family.* Not a word that con-
notes politics, or the organizations which "do" politics. The
same word the Manson clan used. The same word the Mafia
uses. A word that implies fierce commitment and ties as thick
as blood.

SELF-DEFENSE

The existence of the hippie/drop-out community represents both an alternative to the present system ...and a means for its destruction. The hip community poses a way of living rather than simply a way of surviving. On the one hand it rejects middle-class values, on the other hand it makes possible a fuller and more complete life. Out of that emerges a revolutionary culture.

This community is not a regional phenomenon--- there is no such thing as a Boston hippie community, a New York hippie community, a San Francisco hippie community. There is one hip community and it spreads and grows from one end of this country to the other.

Our need and desire for our own community and for the right to discover our own forms of living are in direct conflict with the basic nature of Amerika today---we become targets for the enforcers of the brutal values and empty aspirations of this society. We are being attacked because we are an alternative/threat and in order to survive we are going to have to defend ourselves and our communities by any means necessary.

We are engaged in a two-fold struggle --- the struggle to create a new way of living, and the struggle to defend ourselves against increasing repression. Already Amerika has determined to prevent our communities from forming, and already we have had to fight back. In the struggle to create our own lives, Self-defense transcends the personal act and becomes an involvement in the communal experience. AS WE FIGHT FOR OUR OWN LIVES WE ARE FIGHTING FOR THE POSSIBILITY OF LIFE...

Our communities must be created and their creation must be defended. We must discover both the forms of living together, and the means of defending these forms together. If we are attacked verbally, we defend ourselves verbally. If we are attacked culturally, we defend ourselves culturally. If we are attacked violently with open hands, we respond violently with open hands. And if we are attacked with weapons, we defend ourselves with weapons.

The idea of self-defense or even violence is not contrary to the idea of love. Our community is not specifically a "love" community, it is a total community. In order to be total we accept all of the elements of living. We don't reject any one element. What we would want, our ideal, is to create the kind of life that doesn't need violence, but at the same time we recognize that in order to be full men no part of life can be rejected.

The hip community is a full community, a culture, a way of life, a way of existing. It's not just a tactic or a ??ans, or another form of pacifism. Many people in ?? hip community are pacific and would not use violence. But there are others of the hip community who know that we must defend those values that we pose as an alternative to Amerika.

The dichotomy is always made between non-violence and violence and that's a false dichotomy. The real difference is between living and death. Some kinds of violence are living, and ?me kinds of violence are death. If our violence ?mes out of our desire to live and is only di- ?ected against those who would prevent us from living, then that is living-violence. If violence, like police and military violence, is directed against the lives of others, then that is death-violence. That's the real dichotomy; living and death, not non-violence and violence...Our com- munity represents living.

WE MUST DEFINE OURSELVES FOR OURSELVES IN THE LANGUAGE AND GESTURES OF OUR OWN DISCOVERIES

WE MUST LEARN TO RECOGNIZE EACH OTHER AND TO KNOW THAT ANYONE WHO IS NOT WITH US IS THE ENEMY

WE MUST LEARN TO FIGHT AS WELL AS SEEK TO LOVE

WE MUST TAKE UP THE GUN AS WELL AS THE JOINT

WE MUST DEFEND OUR COMMUNITY AND OUR OWN HUMANITY

'We're looking for people who like to draw'

up against the wall/

341 EAST 10th St.   LOWER EAST

Page created by the Motherfuckers for "The Rat," underground newspaper with an office on the Lower East Side.

ARMED LOVE

The first Motherfucker action in which we claimed our unspeakable name took place on February 12, 1968, a little over a year after my arrest in St. Patrick's Cathedral. Continuing the attack on cultural icons that had been part of the strategy of Angry Arts week, we chose as our target Lincoln Center for the Performing Arts.

The Lower East Side was in the grip of a garbage strike. The streets were ripe. Mountains of plastic bags filled with uncollected refuse piled up on the sidewalks. Rats grew fat and numerous. Meanwhile, on the Upper West Side of Manhattan, Lincoln Center sparkled, with every one of its windows washed and every marble step swept. Our action was simple. We collected bags of garbage and loaded them into a car. One person drove them to our prearranged meeting place. The rest of us marched through the streets to the subway and boarded the uptown train, pounding on pots, shaking tambourines, humming into kazoos and blowing on pennywhistles the entire way. Ben carried a black flag on a pole and handed out fliers to our fellow subway riders, who did their best to pretend we didn't exist. At 66th Street and Broadway, we dashed onto the platform, ran up the stairs, met the car that was carrying the garbage, loaded it into a wheeled canvas post office cart, and marched off to the Center. A phalanx of security guards blocked our entrance to the buildings.

We deposited the mess on the marble steps in front of them and handed out the remainder of our fliers. Uniformed police arrived and formed a cordon between the building and us. As we marched back to the subway, plainclothes police followed us. When we stopped for coffee at a cafeteria, they eyed us from an adjoining table. One cop, more undercover than the rest, sat down with us and tried uncomfortably to strike up a conversation. Ben reached over and gave him a friendly pat on his shoulder as if to say: "Nice try buddy." Then it was back to the ghetto for fierce and energetic discussions about the meaning of what we had just done.*

The text of the flier we handed out was my first Motherfucker manifesto.

WE PROPOSE A CULTURE EXCHANGE
(garbage for garbage)
AMERICA TURNS THE WORLD INTO GARBAGE
IT TURNS ITS GHETTOES INTO GARBAGE
IT TURNS VIETNAM INTO GARBAGE
IN THE NAME OF UNIVERSAL PRINCIPLES
(DEMOCRACY HUMAN RIGHTS)
IN THE NAME OF THE FATHERLAND
(COLLIE DOGS NEW ENGLAND CHURCHES)
IN THE NAME OF MAN   IN THE NAME OF ART
AMERICA TAKES
ALL THAT IS EDIBLE, EXCHANGEABLE, INVESTABLE
AND LEAVES THE REST

THE WORLD IS OUR GARBAGE, WE SHALL NOT WANT. WE
LIE DOWN IN
GREEN PASTURES—THE REST LIE IN GARBAGE

---

* Newsreel made a short documentary entitled, of course, "Garbage." This is the only Motherfucker action documented on film.

AND WE PLAY AS WE MAKE OUR GARBAGE
BEETHOVEN, BACH, MOZART, SHAKESPEARE
TO COVER THE SOUND OF OUR GARBAGE MAKING

AND WE EXCLUDE THE GARBAGE FROM OUR PALACES OF
CULTURE
AND WE SHALL NOT ALLOW IT TO MARRY OUR
DAUGHTERS
AND WE WILL NOT NEGOTIATE WITH IT OR LET IT TAKE
OUR SHIPS

BUT WE ARE FACED WITH A REVOLT OF THE GARBAGE
A CULTURAL REVOLUTION
GARBAGE FERTILIZES
DISCOVERS ITSELF

AND WE OF THE LOWER EAST SIDE HAVE DECIDED TO
BRING THIS CULTURAL REVOLUTION TO LINCOLN
CENTER—IN BAGS

IS NOT LINCOLN CENTER WHERE IT BELONGS.

Below the manifesto we told people where to assemble and
signed off with:

UP AGAINST THE WALL MOTHER*FUCKER
and into the trashcan

Like the disruption of St. Patrick's Cathedral, our Lincoln
Center action inspired a pornographic fantasy that I recorded
in my journal. I compared the Lincoln Center to Jacqueline
Kennedy's panties, into which modern art fit like "the hand

of her hairdresser." It needed to be "scum cleansed by violent intrusions."

The production of art for consumption by a leisured audience is a bankrupt activity. That had been a premise of Angry Arts week. But the Motherfuckers, under Ben's leadership, quickly developed a vision in which the emphasis shifted from war on cultural institutions to total war on The System. By "The System," we meant more than the economic and political institutions by which the rich wage unequal war against the poor, stealing the fruits of their labors, and despoiling the earth in the process. We meant the totality of reality as shaped by, dependent upon, and supportive of those institutions. We meant presidents and penises, the Pentagon and our parents, desires and disaffections, torturers and toothpaste.

We set out to organize our base within the counter-culture. If we were "a street gang with an analysis" our analysis was simple: The dropouts flooding into the ghetto were vulnerable. Their naive faith in love and good vibes did not prepare them for survival on the mean streets. They needed protection. Love needed to arm itself. We advocated a politics of rage and tribal bonding, "flower power" as one of our fliers put it, "with thorns." The hippies who were getting most of the media attention extolled an amorphous all-inclusive being, a soft swooning dissolution of the ego. They called it "love." "Love, love, love," they chanted at Be-ins in Central Park, swaying dreamily like seaweed floating in the warm currents of an ethereal sea. They thrust flowers into gun barrels of the soldiers protecting the Pentagon from anti-war protestors. They told the cops they loved them as batons descended on their heads. They proclaimed this love to be the true alternative to all the warring and unhappiness of the dominant culture. They danced its praise with loose, long hair and flowing garments. They invited all those straight square folks with button-down personalities to join the dance. We Motherfuckers liked the dance, but worried that the dancers were weak and didn't know it. We prowled the sidelines and talked of rage—its reality in us and the dangerous rage of society against us.

* * *

The crisis of the Sixties was experienced differently in different sectors of society. For white America it took the form of a children's revolt that tore the culture apart along generational lines.

Adolescence is a time of aching awareness of the gulf between the self and society's expectations. Societies depend for their continued stability on limiting the arc of adolescent discontent. In the Sixties that arc became abnormally extended. Children saw the family as the modular cell out of which the whole oppressive body politic was constructed.

Adolescents rebelled in droves. America offered them a limited menu of acceptable adult roles: they could join the army and become cannon fodder; they could be housewives, office drones, or flunkies in some menial depressing job. None of them looked appetizing. The Sixties was not a time of economic scarcity. Fear of poverty was an insufficient whip to keep young people on the path. Chanting "Hell no! We won't go!" they would change what it meant to grow up or they would not grow up at all.

The traditional rhetoric of the left did not recognize the categories of experience that had driven young people to drop out, and it could not name the goal of their journey The System had produced a murderous war in Vietnam, which gobbled up young people and spit out corpses at a terrifying rate. But it had also produced a slew of seemingly trivial indignities, which, for the dropouts of the Lower East Side, had simply become intolerable.

Communists believe that the working class will be the vanguard of revolution once workers realize they are being exploited and that the exploitation of their labor is the root of all other forms of oppression. The civil rights movement forced the white left to recognize that racism cut across divisions of class, and had burrowed deep into the psyche of the nation. But how was the left to understand the oppression of the privileged white children of America? What "ism" applied to them? They got stoned on acid, listened to rock and roll, came from various classes of society. They revolted against The System—not the "capitalist" system, or the "racist" system, but simply "The System." All of it. The whole kit and caboodle. They could not define their exploitation primarily in terms of their work life. What work? They scrounged and panhandled for a living. They had "white skin privilege." And still they wanted out—out of their families; their schools; their jobs; out of the blond, bovine stupidity of truck stop, Doggie Diner America.

But where was "out"? And what did they find when they got there? The Motherfuckers set out to fill the empty space of "out" with countercultural institutions. "All power to the People" was the Black Panther's slogan. Our less than stirring contribution was "All space to the spaced."

By the beginning of 1968, we had become a formidable presence on the Lower East Side. We ran free stores and crash pads. We organized community feasts in the courtyard of St. Marks Church. We propagandized against the merchandising of hip culture and shook down the psychedelic stores for contributions to our cause. We scammed and shoplifted.

Communists took jobs in factories, to be close to "the people." Motherfuckers hung out on the streets to be close to *our* people, the "freaks" as we fondly called them. Communists went to work. We did as little work as possible. We roamed the streets in dirty black leather jackets, carrying in our pockets thin single blade "K-9" folding knives which we practiced whipping out and flipping open with one hand. The knives made a satisfying click when the blade locked into place.

The center of our universe was the sidewalk in front of Gem's Spa, a narrow little magazine shop with a soda counter on the corner of St. Marks Place and 2nd Avenue. We'd hang out, distribute leaflets, pick up the gossip of the street, then head back to our cluttered store front office on 9th Street opposite Tompkins Square Park, where we churned out a raging flood of flyers on our cranky Gestetner mimeograph machine. The tone of our manifestoes was uncompromising and apocalyptic.

We urged our freak constituency to make love, but prepare for war:

IN REVOLT ONE WINS OR DIES—BUT NO SUICIDES

DIG where it's at: They would like to obliterate us

They think it's us or them (and they're right).
Sitting on the stoop to them is a revolutionary act. You are Che Guevara if you stand on the corner. WE ARE INVOLVED IN A WAR OF SURVIVAL THIS IS A CIVIL WAR AND THERE ARE NO CIVIL RIGHTS We must become a guerrilla stoned army of the streets. DIG: amerika will become a sea of violence in which we will have to swim. Unfortunately people who do not swim will drown.

WE WILL USE THE BUDDY SYSTEM-GANG UP

We must get together in groups each member of which we
know and trust. We must plan ahead.
We must be cool Time is on our side.
Those who are really into shit will not talk about it on the
street
They'll be too busy.

WE ARE ALIVE AND WE MUST STAY ALIVE
THE PIG IS A DEAD ANIMAL

We celebrated our emerging power. This battle cry was
illustrated with a graphic of a gigantic fly:[7]

When the vast body moves thru battlefield streets
it walks on many legs
hungry cells and angry belly
guts of anger/blood of anger
anger in the one fantastic throat that cries:
"Now! Now this body sees, this body knows and aches,
this body will suffer to be chained no more!"
and when the vast body moves thru battlefield streets
the great buildings tremble . . .

When the police harassed our people we called for militant
demonstrations:

They're busting again

IS IT HOT-BECAUSE THE MAN IS UP TIGHT OR IS THE MAN
UP TIGHT BECAUSE IT IS HOT? . . . 6 GIRLS PICKED UP ON
ST. MARX FOR LOOKING YOUNG—ITS AGAINST THE LAW TO
BE YOUNG IN THIS COUNTRY—ITS WITHIN THE LAW TO BE A
FAT OLD PIG BUT WE'RE TELLING YOU—DON'T PUSH MOTH-

ERFUCKER—HANDS OFF MOTHERFUCKER—DON'T SHOVE
MOTHERFUCKER IF YOU SHOVE US WE WILL LEARN TO
SHOVE BACK—IF YOU PUSH US WE WILL LEARN TO PUSH
BACK IF YOU DON'T TAKE YOUR HANDS OFF US WE WILL
PUT OUR HANDS ON—GARBAGE CANS—MATCHES—
OTHER THINGS—IF YOU DON'T RESPECT US—WE WON'T
RESPECT YOU—or YOU'RE PROPERTY! WHAT DOES A PIG
LOOK LIKE RUNNIN SCARED EVER SEE A BOTTLED PIG? WE
DEMAND: STOP HASSLING YOUNG GIRLS AND BOYS STOP
BUSTING YOUNG PEOPLE WHO WANT TO LIVE TOGETHER
AND ARE SICK OF YOUR BOURGEOIS FAMILIES THAT HAVE
MADE US SICK—STOP BUSTING OR WE WILL BUST BACK
THIS IS A NEW BREED OF FLOWER CHILD VENUS PIG TRAP
WE ARE VIOLENT FLOWERS—CACTUS, THORNS
BE IN THE STREET TONITE

And in a similar vein:

LAST NIGHT THE MAN BUSTED ONE OF OUR CRASHPADS
IT WAS <u>CLEAN</u>. (THE MAN LOVES CLEANLINESS)
WITH SORROW WE HAD EXCLUDED OUR BROTHERS THE
RUNAWAYS AND OUR BEAUTIFUL DRUGS (THE MAN DOES
NOT LOVE THEM AND HAS MADE LAWS AGAINST THEM)

BUT-THERE IS NO PLEASING THE MAN—HE BUSTED ANYWAY
(MOVED IN THRU THE DOORS AND WINDOWS) TORE THE
APARTMENT TO PIECES, RIPPED UP FURNITURE, THREW
CLOTHES AROUND, ARRESTED 10 PEOPLE)
            X—ITS GETTING HOT—X—X
DRIVEN MAD BY THE DEATH OF HIS POLITICIANS, SEEING
IN OUR EYES THE REVELATION OF HIS OWN INSANITY, HE
WANTS US OUT OF HIS CITIES BEFORE THE SUMMER STARTS
BUT LISTEN MAN—WE CAME OUT OF YOUR FAT ASS SUBURBS

WE KNOW WHAT YOU SHORT HAIRS ARE LIKE
WE'VE LIVED IN YOUR HOMES
WE'VE HAD YOU FOR FATHERS AND MOTHERS
WERE NOT GOING BACK
WE NEED SPACE—
YOU PUSH US OUT OF OUR PADS SO YOU CAN BUST US IN THE
STREETS—IT WON'T WORK—WE'RE HERE LIKE ROACHES
STOP HASSLING US—

We would riot, throw rocks through the windows of the bank opposite Gem's Spa, and run through the streets chased by beat cops from the 9th precinct reinforced by the Tactical Patrol Force. Those of us they caught got dragged to jail. Those of us who escaped rushed to our storefront to churn out fliers calling for new demonstrations, which would invariably result in more riots and more arrests. And more fliers. We celebrated our battles with hymns to liberation:

LIBERATION IN THE STREETS

Happened because a crash pad was busted—but also for its own sake. The breaking into the crash pad was a cause and an opportunity—an opportunity to liberate a form of energy and a form of life that can not be coopted and turned against us. While the rest tremble we look forward to the heat of summer.

We expect the police to be brutal as we expect someone who stubs his toe to cry out—America stubs its toe—looks down—and there we are in the street—which is where we belong. We have many new slogans. Among them are: <u>The streets belong to the people and the people belong in the streets</u>. And: <u>Up against the wall Motherfucker</u>. People call us suicidal sidewalk psychopaths. The first young unprotected bud pushing thru the soil in Spring

is suicidal—its safer not trying to grow. And it's Spring.
And we're pushing.

Flush from our confrontations we exulted:

NOW WE KNOW FOR SURE:
THE STREETS WILL BE OURS—
THE FROZEN FILTHY STREAM
MELTS AND A LIBERATED FLOOD POURS THRU THE STREET—
UPROOTING/OVERTURNING—
THE STREETS ARE OUR BATTLEFIELD
THEY ARE THE GARDENS WHERE WE WILL LIBERATE
NEW FORMS OF LIFE
WHERE A NEW RACE OF MEN IS LEARNING TO BE HUMAN—
LEARNING TO FIGHT
LEARNING TO LIVE
THE STREETS BELONG TO THE PEOPLE—AND THE
PEOPLE BELONG IN THE STREETS!

I lived for those moments of mingled fear and exhilaration, when we stopped playing by the rules. Running in the streets regardless of lights and traffic, fighting with the police, hearing glass breaking felt like the very essence of freedom. It seemed so enticingly simple: all that was needed to be free was to refuse to obey. Of course, "The System" would respond by trying to crush us and force us back within the lines. The trick was to enlarge the space between our challenge and its response.

The charge of the bull is the moment of truth for the matador. He emerges triumphant, humiliated—or dead. Our moment of truth came when the sirens wailed and the police pulled out their billyclubs.

We believed we were inventing a new way to be white revolutionaries in America. We were willing to take risks, to abandon all privilege. Even the New Left, as it was formulating itself in the SDS chapters of college campuses across the country, seemed too tame and tentative for us. No more dithering and prevarication. It was time to put up or shut up.

BREAKING THE MORAL CALLUS

For a few brief years we were incandescent. We would burn the armor off the body politic. Naked ourselves, we would grasp the naked truth and live in her embrace.

The world was gripped by a vast instability. Geysers were bursting through hard rock. Wounds that never healed were opening. Cleansing waves were washing through the halls of history, jumbling the furniture, tumbling closets full of secrets, freeing those trapped beneath the floorboards. Terrible crimes were being exposed. We would ride the waves. No, we would *be* the wave, and not just the wave, but the spume at its leading edge.

The Lower East Side was our home turf, but we aspired to act on a world stage. We were small in numbers. We had a narrow base of support. We were contemptuous of the timidity of the organizers of the large mobilizations we attended, but incapable of organizing anything on a comparable scale. We would lead by example.

In October 1967, a major demonstration against the war in Vietnam culminated in an encirclement of the Pentagon. The National Mobilization Committee to End the War in Vietnam ("the Mobe") planned for protestors to engage in decorous non-violent civil disobedience. Abbie Hoffman and Jerry Rubin let it be known that a pentagon was the sign of the devil and that they intended to conduct an exorcism at the conclusion of which the Pentagon would levitate off the ground. The Motherfuckers had not yet fully coalesced as a group but Ben and those of us from the Lower East Side who went with him were in no mood for such frivolity. On the day of the demonstration, Ben joined a self-proclaimed Revolutionary Contingent of militants that tore down a chain link fence and charged toward the building, only to be beaten by a phalanx of federal marshals. Undeterred, a small group, waiving the flag of the Vietnamese National Liberation Front, with Ben in the forefront, ran towards a temporarily unguarded side entrance and dashed inside, where they were met by a solid wall of soldiers who beat them back out the door. But they had done it! They had penetrated into the actual belly of the beast.[8]

The following month the Foreign Policy Association held a banquet for Secretary of State Dean Rusk at the New York Hilton. We bought cows blood at a butcher shop, filled plastic bags with the stuff, concealed the bags in our pockets, and traveled uptown to meet the invitees. We had helped circulate a flier that read:

> **The Forces of liberation (**feeling that there is enough pollution in our city already without adding a Secretary of State): Hereby Announce that DEAN RUSK has been denied permission to enter New York City for any purpose whatsoever. ▬▬▬▬▬ Despite this he intends to accept an award at a Foreign Policy Assoc. dinner . . . <u>The forces of liberation </u>are therefore compelled to urge all their supporters to assemble in front of the hotel . . . to welcome him appropriately.

As guests pulled up to the entrance and liveried bellhops rushed to hold open the doors of their limousines, we hurled our bags of blood, splattering evening dresses and tuxedos. I have a photograph taken at the riot that followed. It shows a policeman standing in a threatening pose over a demonstrator who is down on the pavement. I am looking on, hands at my side. I make no gesture to intervene.

Martin Luther King was assassinated on April 4, 1968. Major riots took place in Baltimore, Boston, Chicago, Detroit, Kansas City, Newark, Washington, DC, and Harlem. Forty-six people died.

Unrest in the streets was spilled over onto campuses across the nation. On April 23, a group of Columbia University students including members of the Student Afro-American Society (SAS), attempted to stop construction of a gymnasium the University was building in Morningside Park. Morningside Park lies on the border between the campus and Harlem. The huge building would swallow precious open space used by the community. Members of the community (predominantly Black) would have some use of the facility, but they would have to enter through a back door. Columbia University students (predominantly White) would enter through the main entrance on the other side. The plan for separate but unequal entrances stank of southern style racism and the community was up in arms. There had been numerous community protests joined by SAS, but construction continued.

Now the issue of the gymnasium would become the spark that ignited the largest protest Columbia had ever seen. Discontent with the university went far beyond its voracious land grabbing. The SAS students were joined by members of SDS, who had been protesting the University's links to the Institute for Defense Analyses, a weapons research program with connections to the Pentagon. Columbia was acting like an arrogant racist slumlord. It was also complicit in the war effort. It provided intellectual cover for war criminals and trained their proxies and facilitators. It expected students to be passive sponges, soaking up the wisdom of their professors. Now all the separate streams of protest against Columbia's policies at home and abroad were about to come together in a mighty river.

When the protestors started to tear down a fence at the gymnasium site, the police moved in, and one person was arrested. The protesters then returned to campus, joined by member of the community, and began an occupation of Hamilton Hall. Dean Coleman was temporarily held hostage in his office. The occupation would soon spread to five other buildings and last a week.

Ten days earlier, Grayson Kirk, President of Columbia, had given a speech in Charlottesville, Virginia. He warned his audience that "young people, in disturbing numbers, appear to reject all forms of authority, from whatever source derived, and . . . have taken refuge in a turbulent and inchoate nihilism whose sole objectives are destruction. I know of no time in our history," he said, "when the gap between the generations has been wider or more potentially dangerous."

Mark Rudd, chairman of Columbia SDS and one of the leaders of the strike, had replied the day before the gymnasium demonstration with an open letter.

> Your charge of nihilism is indeed ominous; for if it were true, our nihilism would bring the whole civilized world, from Columbia to Rockefeller Center, crashing down upon all our heads. . . . You are quite right in feeling that the situation is "potentially dangerous" for if we win, we will take control of your world, your corporation, your University and attempt to mold a world in which we and other people can live as human beings. . . . We will have to destroy at times, even vio-

lently, in order to end your power and your system—
but that is a far cry from nihilism. . . .

You call for order in respect for authority; we
call for justice, freedom, and socialism."

He concluded:

There is only one thing left to say. It may sound nihilis-
tic to you, since it is the opening shot in the war of
liberation. I'll use the words of LeRoi Jones, whom I'm
sure you don't like a whole lot: "Up against the wall,
motherfucker this is a stick up."[9]

Reminiscing later, Mark wrote:

Perhaps nothing upset our enemies more than this slogan. To them it seemed to show the extent to which
we had broken with their norms, how far we had sunk
to brutality, hatred and obscenity. Great! The New
York Times put forward three interpretations of the
slogan, the only one of which I remember is the one
which had to do with putting the administration up
against the wall before a firing squad—apparently our
fascistic 'final solution.' The truth is almost as bad: the
slogan defined Grayson Kirk, David Truman, the
Trustees, many of the faculty, and the cops as our enemies. Liberal solutions, 'restructuring', partial
understandings, compromise are not allowed anymore. The essence of the matter is that we are out for
social and political revolution."[10]

That Mark picked up on the rhetoric of the Motherfuckers
was not fortuitous. Mark had seen Ben and a cohort of Moth-

erfuckers disrupt an SDS convention by shouting at speakers with whom we disagreed, "That's bullshit and you know it." He liked the phrase. After the convention he had hung out with us a bit on the Lower East Side. He was impressed by our impatience with theory and influenced by our reliance on the vivifying effect of action in the streets to draw converts to our cause. In Columbia SDS he formed an "action faction," in opposition to the "praxis axis" whose members talked Marxist theory and believed in the need to educate people before they could act. Mark had gone to Cuba, and willingly admitted to being an adherent of the cult of Che. He read Regis Debray's "*Revolution in the Revolution,*" which argued that the revolution begins with the armed struggle of small bands of guerrillas. In Mark's head Che, Debray, and the Motherfuckers were all singing the same song: Action itself is educational.

When we heard about the strike, we traveled uptown to participate. We arrived at Hamilton Hall where round the clock meetings were taking place. Differences in the styles of organizing between the Blacks and White students soon emerged. Rumors spread that some members of the Black community had brought in guns. The rumors were true.[11] The white student leadership was not ready for armed struggle. The leadership of the Blacks in Hamilton asked the white students to leave. They could take over other buildings if they wished. Most of them complied. But Charlie Motherfucker at first refused. As a true Motherfucker he was unwilling to be categorized as less militant than anyone. Mark Motherfucker, who stayed with Charlie, remembers him responding to the demand that he leave with, "Go fuck yourself. You punk bourgeois Blacks, you don't know anything. I've got some friends here and I'm staying."

I left and joined a group of white students heading for Low

Library, which housed Grayson Kirk's office. A bench was rammed through a pane of glass on a side door, demonstrators poured in, and after a brief hesitation forced the door to the president's office. One of the most famous photographs of the Columbia occupation shows the poet, David Shapiro, sitting at the president's desk wearing dark glasses and smoking one of his Cuban cigars. Meanwhile other students rifled through his files for evidence of the University's connections to the Pentagon. Mark Motherfucker recalls David handed him the first cigar he ever smoked.

Sometime later, word came down that a bust was imminent. Many students jumped out windows to escape. When the police did arrive, they marched in, took custody of Kirk's Rembrandt, locked his inner offices and left a rump group of about twelve protestors sitting in a circle holding a meeting.[12]

Mark, who had left and then returned recalls:

> We [Johnny, Steve, and Mark Motherfucker] got there and they were having this discussion. They were in the Secretary's area of the president's office and the door was locked to the president's office and there was a discussion at the time "do we take over the president's office." And it was like a long drawn out discussion and went on and on for hours. Johnny goes "I think we can get in there," and we start looking around and it turns out there was this coffee pot with a hot plate and there was a little door so the president didn't have to leave his office and could reach out to get his coffee and they slid me through, I being the skinniest one and I opened the door next to it and Johnny and Steve and I now occupied the president's office. So we go to the other door, the one that leads to the Secretary's office, which is where they're having this meeting and Johnny

opens the door and sticks his head out and goes "hi" and they go we just had a vote not to take over that office. No problem says Johnny this is a separate occupation. He said only women are allowed to use the bathroom. So about 10 minutes later there is a knock on the door. "We voted to take over this office."[13]

From Low, Ben and the majority of the Motherfuckers moved on to the Mathematics Building, which was quickly transformed into a reasonable facsimile of a Lower East Side crash pad. Lecture halls became communal living spaces strewn with piles of clothing, remnants of meals, backpacks, and bedding. Blackboards that had been covered with equations now sprouted slogans—Up Against the Wall prominent among them—and drafts for manifestoes. Wooden partitions between toilet stalls were torn down to build barricades. Those who needed privacy were having problems.

Men and women used the same bathrooms, slept in their clothing, and stopped caring how they smelled. And of course there were endless meetings to discuss strategy and tactics.

Tom Hayden chaired most of the meetings. We Motherfuckers were impatient with all the talk, although film footage taken during the occupation shows John Motherfucker getting himself elected to some position or other that I can no longer remember.

When word reached us that athletes and fraternity boys had formed a ring around Low Library and were refusing to let anyone in or out of the building we climbed out of the windows of Math and marched to Low carrying boxes of groceries. The blockaders were clean cut, shorthaired, and beefy. They didn't look like us. One might have thought that, separated by oceans of ideology, long hairs and short hairs were evolving into different species. We called them "jocks."

They called us "pukes." We marched a few times outside their perimeter and then suddenly, Ben in the lead, made a rush to break through their line. Fights broke out. We were pushed back. Terrified as usual, I lagged behind, and managed to avoid the worst of it.

Ben was primarily concerned with organizing our defense against the inevitable assault by the police. Every floor was barricaded with furniture. He remembers piling heavy desks in the stairwell, with wedges under them so they could easily be tipped down the steps onto police coming from below. We ran soapy water down seven flights of polished concrete steps so the cops would lose their footing.

The cops moved in after midnight. They moved from building to building, saving Math for last. When word reached us that our time was approaching, John recalls thinking the cops might try a sneak attack through a tunnel in the basement that connected Math to adjacent buildings. He remembers "shoving desks, chairs, garbage cans and a lone Coke machine into the tunnel's entrance," to create a blockade, followed, when we realized it wasn't enough, by the marble partitions that separated the stalls of what had once been the basement men's room.

For John Motherfucker, the tearing down of the partitions carried the symbolism of the struggle, which ultimately was about the breaking down of all restraints and barriers. He wrote:

> We ripped out the partitions that created the stalls that separated the shittees who had always come down from the classrooms above and defined the divisions between all the Math syntheses and formulations and logarithms and the graphs of generations of conceptual scholars seeking privacy for a moment between

the stall-walls of these individual retreat bowls where the functions of life could be integrated with the abstractions. . . . Those stall walls came down. And the cries rang out,

"WE ARE ALL ANTI-PARTITIONALISTS"
"DOWN WITH THE WALLS"
"LIBERATE THE STALLS."

And on that night, while all of us were getting busted and beaten, Freedom reigned among the toilets of Math.[14]

For the Motherfuckers the "issues" that had sparked the takeover were secondary. We were the vanguard of the new order, vandals of liberation, sworn enemies of all hierarchical institutions. We were contemptuous of all those who accepted roles within those institutions, students and faculty alike. We distrusted all intellectual activity that was not devoted to revolution, all thought divorced from action, all rationality that shut itself off from the surrealism of the unconscious. We had no respect for institutions of "higher" learning that shelter those within them from the "lower" learning of the street. We came to tear down the walls, not to repair them.

Math had a reputation for militancy, partly because of our presence there. Many expected we would get the worst of it. Memories of how the bust actually came down vary. Ben recalls that the cops couldn't get through our barricades and we negotiated our surrender. A woman on the fourth floor recalls hearing the cops shout and curse and an ax crashing through the door of the fourth floor room in which she and about twenty other protestors were huddled. She saw blood on the steps as she was being hauled away. I remember little except that I emerged unscathed. Perhaps the police had saved Math for last partly because of our reputation for militancy and had already vented most, but not all, of their fury on protestors in other buildings by the time they got to us. Some of us got beat. I was just lucky.

* * *

My brother Michael was a student at Columbia. He had been one of the founding members of Columbia SDS. Mark Rudd was his roommate. Michael dropped in at Low Library twice, but otherwise did not participate in the occupations. He agreed with Herbert that universities, whatever their shortcomings, were realms of comparative freedom, and therefore disrupting them was counter-productive. The university had not been a realm of freedom for me. I was done with academia. I returned to Columbia not to follow in Franz's footsteps, but to disrupt the institution where he had taught so brilliantly. First his home, now his university: Once again, I was contaminating the refuge of reason.

Michael and I had never been close as children. He was eight years younger than I. He had observed my fearsome battles with my mother and decided to keep his distance. After Columbia, we went our separate ways and remained estranged for most of the Sixties. Sometime after Columbia he wrote me a scathing letter:

> You know what I have to say. It is that when all your motherfuckering is gone, when new language that is fake, new community that is not community, human liberation that is not liberation, new life that is not life, fighting that is not fighting, when all that is gone, I will remain, and with me will remain people who never

pretended to be more whole than they were, or to give
more than they could give, and who knew that courage
and free spirit come at the end of the line, not the
beginning . . . These people, not you, will be the revolutionaries . . . They will not pretend that they hate the
cops or the corporations, they will not be transfigured
into your images. They will be transfigured and still
remain ordinary—they won't live in orgasm. Neither
will you. We don't live in such a world.

He was merciless on what he saw as the distorted psychological origins of my politics:

Twenty-years of sniveling and humiliation everywhere,
in school, in stores, groveling and full of hate . . . at
your father and your mother and your stepfather, per-
secuted all the time, pathetic . . . hurt, clinging to
sexuality, torturing yourself and other people—but
never with satisfaction! You think that you are big
enough to tear all that apart and remake the world,
that suddenly it is you alone who knows how to live
and fuck, that we are all castrated party hacks! WHO
is arrogant?

Nor did he have patience with my conflicted relation to rationality, a legacy I could never completely disown or embrace:

Take the specter of rationality and kick it around
some more first until you are not afraid of it, until you
realize it isn't what you thought it was . . . Reason isn't
to whip people with, neither is what you do. Reason
isn't a thing at all, forget it. It means doing things
right.

Years later, Michael later wrote a book, *What's Left?* in which my Motherfuckeresque life style politics is blamed for the demise of a genuinely effective radical movement. Perhaps he's more right than I could admit at the time. Perhaps we did get a bit carried away. But I suspect that revolutionary periods, and particularly aborted revolutions, are always messy affairs, combining sense and non-sense, the heroic and ridiculous, in unequal measure.

* * *

At its founding convention in 1962, Students for a Democratic Society ratified a declaration of principles that became known as the Port Huron Statement.[15] The Statement was "an effort in understanding and changing the conditions of humanity in the late twentieth century, an effort rooted in the ancient, still unfulfilled conception of man attaining determining influence over his circumstances of life." It marked the birth of a "new left" intent on remaking the language and practice of politics. "Our work," it proclaimed "is guided by the sense that we may be the last generation in the experiment with living." It acknowledged that many white college students had grown up comfortably in the richest nation on earth. It listed the factors that were undermining that comfortable existence:

> As we grew . . . our comfort was penetrated by events too troubling to dismiss. First, the permeating and victimizing fact of human degradation, symbolized by the Southern struggle against racial bigotry, compelled most of us from silence to activism. Second, the enclosing fact of the Cold War, symbolized by the presence of the Bomb, brought awareness that we our-

selves, and our friends, and millions of abstract "others" we knew more directly because of our common peril, might die at any time.

The apparent apathy of most Americans was a "glaze over deeply felt anxieties." The problem that would have to be addressed in awakening Americans to the urgent peril was that "[a] shell of moral callus separates the citizen from sensitivity to the common peril: this is the result of a lifetime saturation with horror."

Despite his disdain for the compromises of student activism, Ben decided that the Motherfuckers should become an official SDS chapter. We believed ourselves well-situated to break "the moral callus"—including the vestiges of that moral callus which restrained the militancy of the movement. Into the sedate halls of the academy we would bring the disruptive style of the streets.

As an SDS chapter we took every opportunity to chastise students for their lack of daring. On one occasion we went to a SDS meeting in the basement of the psychology building at Columbia University. The students talked on and on and we became impatient. I drifted away from the discussion. Exploring the corridors, I discovered a hall lined with cages full of pigeons that were used in behavioral experiments. Grabbing hold of a cage I carried it back to the room where the meeting was taking place. Propaganda of the deed! I released the pigeons from their little prisons, shouting something appropriate. As I ran out of the meeting the puzzled birds, wheeled about the room, banged into windows, and flapped down the corridors. I learned later that I had destroyed months of some professor's research. Did I care? There was only one task worthy of my devotion—total liberation. There was only one experiment worthy of respect—the complete transformation of the System.

In 1968 we traveled to a SDS national convention in Michigan. I seized the microphone during an interminable debate between non-ideological new lefties and the Maoist Progressive Labor Party faction. Dropping my pants, with my penis flapping in the wind, I condemned intellectual masturbation. Our role as apostles from the street to the student movement was not to argue ideology, but to instill into the movement's moribund theoretical discussions the urgency and anarchy of the streets. Our "Chapter Report" on the convention was a succinct expression of our point.

> A MOLOTOV COCKTAIL
> IS A BOTTLE FILLED WITH
> THREE PARTS KEROSENE
> AND ONE PART MOTOR OIL
> IT IS CAPPED
> AND WRAPPED
> WITH COTTON
> SOAKED WITH GASOLINE
> TO USE—
> LIGHT COTTON
> THROW BOTTLE
> FIRE AND EXPLOSION OCCUR
> ON IMPACT WITH TARGET
>
> A "WHITE RADICAL"
> IS THREE PARTS BULLSHIT
> AND ONE PART HESITATION.
>
> IT IS NOT REVOLUTIONARY
> AND SHOULD NOT BE
> STOCKPILED
> AT THIS TIME

respectfully submitted

UP AGAINST THE WALL
MOTHERFUCKER

The students whose timidity we condemned were often suitably impressed by our militancy. The vanguard of the movement belonged to those who were willing to take life and death risks. SDS organizers made pilgrimages to our crashpads. Some of them later joined the Weathermen, which went through its own distinctly Motherfuckeresque stage before it disappeared underground. At one Weathermen gathering Bernadine Dorn saluted the crowd with three raised fingers symbolizing the carving fork the Manson gang stuck in the belly of the victims in the Tate/LaBianca murder spree. When Susan Atkins, one of his gang, was sitting in jail, she blithely confessed to one of her cellmates that she had murdered Sharon Tate. The cellmate was horrified and asked why she'd done it. She replied, "We wanted to do a crime that would shock the world, that the world would have to stand up and take notice."[16] The desire to shock the world, to make it stand up and take notice was widespread at the time.

THE LIBERATION OF FANTASY

At 89 East 10th Street on March 21 [1967] from about 5 pm the UAWMF [Up Against the Wall Motherfuckers] held a 24-hour Spring Feast. Leaflets advertising this event had been circulated throughout the East Village area for some two weeks and at about 9 pm there were about 100 people at the four-floor derelict apartment house.

Our source states that the place was filthy, there were no lights, illumination being provided by candles and by battery operated lanterns.

Entrance to the building was made either from a store front, slightly below street level, or on the first floor which is some eight steps above street level. On entering by the store front our source went through into the "kitchen" and found a mess of food, a flooded sink and an exit to an enclosed back yard which was filled with rubbish and garbage. Source reported a m/f couple on the floor in the passageway, covered by a blanket having sexual intercourse.

On the first floor a "band" had been formed using bottles, garbage can lids, a broken chair, and various noise makers as instruments. People were milling around and several m/f's (male/females) were asleep on the floor, indicating drug abuse—

On the second floor the scene was repeated, with the exception that the band was missing, replaced by a simple "light show." During the period 10-12, several acts of sexual intercourse were observed and acts of sexual perversion.

Of the 100 people in the building our source estimates that seventy were males, equally divided between Negro and Caucasian races; of the thirty or so girls, only three were Negro.

—*Surveillance report of an undercover New York City police officer*[17]

As a longhaired, dirty Motherfucker I looked in the mirror and saw, with some satisfaction, my mother's worst nightmare.

The Motherfuckers allowed me to rant and rave as I never had before. My anger at The System—its war, its racism, its total vile hypocrisy—was real. My motherfuckering wasn't just psychodrama even if the anger I expressed was fueled by pent up frustrations of my childhood. I found release from my painful introversion in action. I was finally clawing through to something real. I wanted to feast on the flesh of life. I was tired of bloodless abstractions. I was a Motherfucker. Our task was to cut through facades, to unveil, to rend, to penetrate.

My mother never appeared in my masturbatory sado-masochistic fantasies, or if she did, it was in deep disguise. But here I was a Motherfucker. The System was our mother and in the revolution we fucked her.

Parental authority is writ large in the coercive authority of the state. In challenging the state it's easy to fall into the role of rebellious child. If society is the parent, and specifically the mother, and we fuck her in anger, or in love, or in some inextricable mix of the two, do we desire to merge with her, to destroy her, or to be destroyed by her?

On the surface our angry, anarchistic counter-cultural take-no-prisoners motherfuckerism was all rage and rejection. But did there lie at its secret core an acceptance of our childishness, a longing for our abusive parent as intense as our rejection of her? Did our politics, despite all our utopian yearnings, betray an inability to imagine taking power from our parent, and ending the subordination of childhood? We could always rely on the state to play the role of dominatrix and beat up on her disobedient children. Our politics was a passion play in which the bad parent proved her meanness, over and over again to our masochistic satisfaction. Did we secretly identify with the hand that beat us?

I now believe that in my fantasy of the abuse heaped on Cardinal Spellman I was both the sodomized choir boys and their sodomizer. In my fantasy of the hand exploring Jacqueline Kennedy's panties, mine was the hand, and also Jacqueline's genitals. And I surmise that my Motherfucker persona concealed a hidden longing to be embraced by what I rejected, and that I experienced the pain of the mother-state's rejection as pleasure.

I have come to believe that these ambiguities are characteristic of a certain style of predominantly male radical politics. It is a politics which, however worthy its goals, is self-defeating and "infantile" in that it repetitively reenacts the relation of child to parent. The parent restrains the child. He throws a tantrum. He beats his little fists bloody against the bars of his crib. He grows up. The bars of his crib become the bars of his prison. He continues to beat his hands bloody. The bars do not bend or even notice.

It is easy to dismiss this politics as nothing more than childish tantrums, and to profess that a baleful acceptance of the status quo is more "mature." It's more difficult to disentangle, delicately, as one would a bird caught in a net, the genuinely radical and uncompromising elements in this politics from those which are self-defeating.

* * *

From my file box of Sixties memorabilia, I extract a yellowing copy of one of my Motherfucker manifestoes:

MANIFESTO

We demand a society for the prevention of cruelty to fantasy. We know that when our society becomes a society for the preservation and procreation of fantasy it will be a good society.

Until then fantasy will be at war with society. Society will attempt the suppression of fantasy, but fantasy will spring up again and again, infecting the youth, waging urban guerrilla warfare, sabotaging the smooth functioning of bureaucracies (waylaying the typist on the way to the water cooler, kidnapping the executive between office and home), creeping into the bedrooms of respectable families, eventually emerging into the streets, taking over the streets, waging pitched battles and winning (its victory is inevitable).

We are the vanguard of fantasy. Where we live is liberated territory in which fantasy moves freely at all hours of the day, from which it mounts attacks on occupied territory. Each day brings new areas under our control. Each day a victory is reported. Each day fantasy discovers new forms of organization. Each day it further consolidates its control, has less to fear, can afford to spend more time in self-discovery. Even in the midst of battles it plans the cities of the future.

We are full of optimism and courage. We relish the future.

The manifesto became a Motherfucker flier illustrated with the repeated image of a snarling baboon. Between the images the phrase: "MY UTOPIA IS AN ENVIRONMENT THAT WORKS SO WELL I CAN RUN WILD IN IT."

Despite the triumphant tone of my homage to fantasy, I had a problem. I did not much like my fantasies. I had less wish to liberate them than to be liberated from them. "All power to the imagination" was a fine slogan, but the imagination does not discriminate. "All power to the pornographic imagination?"—would that be an appropriate revolutionary slogan? Charles Manson acted out the fantasies I confined to paper. Bernadine Dohrn, with her three-finger salute, paid homage to him. If the System was an obscenity and our fantasy was obscene, were we fighting fire with fire or adding to the blaze?

For all my militancy, I worried that my fantasy life was viscous and reactionary. I could not reconcile the contradiction between the revolutionary and pornographic imagination, between what I believed was my genuine passion for justice with my equally compelling obsessions. I worried not so much about "cruelty to fantasy" as about the cruelty of my fantasies in which violence, including sexual violence, anger, and shit were identified with the forces of liberation.

Sometimes my fantasy life found expression in lighthearted provocations. On one occasion, I collected donations for the rent on our store front by carrying an empty toilet bowl up and down St. Marks Place shouting "America shits money. Shit here." A crowd gathered. Officer Rainey arrived and demanded I hand over the plumbing. The crowd chanted "Free the toilet! Free the toilet! I placed it gingerly in a trash container, where Rainey beat it to death with his nightstick. When he was done smashing it to pieces, he turned to me in a fury and snarled: "That trash basket is for trash, but not for your kind of trash." Then he arrested me. For littering.

The toilet bust was fun, but the deeper levels of my fantasy did not lend themselves to comedy. They were the source of a steady stream of quasi-political violent and pornographic musings. I wrote:

> [A]ggression must now be an ethereal pus, swelling the membrane of America, a bloody ejaculated sperm on the street.
> . . . The peace movement must become a sex crime.

> . . . We are attempting to create a liberated zone, to clear a space for ourselves, to build in it alternate institutions, in order that we may stay alive. But we can also be vitalized by the discovery that there is no way to live, that we are offered only alternative ways of

dying . . . If we decide that society has linked for us freedom and death, then we can play with liberation only when we play with death: at demonstrations. Our liberation will be splashing about in a blood bath . . .

Unlike the Motherfuckers, who were always in battle mode, both Abbie Hoffman and Jerry Rubin played the revolution for laughs. Prancing in front of television cameras they acted the part of revolutionaries having fun playing at being revolutionaries. The revolution *would* be televised. Revolutionaries would become media personalities. The media was there to be manipulated. It had to be seduced into spreading subversive messages. The first rule for revolutionary engagement with the media was unpredictability: dance between seriousness and put on; invent realities on the spur of the moment; keep them guessing; charm, beguile, threaten, and disrupt; turn politics into a theater of the absurd.

There was, of course, a price to pay for all that media attention. The paradox of serious revolutionaries playing at being revolutionaries who believed that play *was* revolutionary tended to collapse into a simple, unparadoxical lack of seriousness. The media invariably extorted its pound of flesh, turning subversion into titillation, subverting the subverters.

We were both envious and contemptuous of the Yippie media stars. We were the antithesis of the Abbie and Jerry show. The media could not speak our name. We clung to the grubby reality of the Lower East Side. The Black Panthers were more our kin than the Yippies. We did not fuck around.

* * *

In the Sixties Black revolutionaries enacted a dangerous pageant of anger and defiance. They costumed themselves for armed struggle in black leather jackets and carried guns. Their performance was greeted with a rain of bullets. They chanted "Off the Pigs!" but more often than not it was the pigs that offed them. The Motherfuckers, under Ben's leadership, insisted that Whites must take the same risks as Blacks. When the Black Panthers held a benefit at Bill Graham's Fillmore East, we leafleted the street with flyers which proclaimed:

WE DON'T SUPPORT THE BLACK STRUGGLE
SUPPORT IS NOT "STRUGGLE"
"SUPPORT" IS THE EVASION OF STRUGGLE

To support is not to understand our own needs for liberation. To support is to remain passive in the struggle for life: it is the failure of whites to see their own being, to see the possibilities of their own humanity. . . . [I]t is only through making our own struggle that we join in common struggle: REVOLUTION.

I passed out fliers side by side with Ben. I could not tell him that the Black Panthers seemed to me to be living in a terrifying corner of reality, where the violence of my fantasy life was realized, and where death was the price of the attempt at liberation.

The atmosphere of the time was ripe with threats and prophecies. Our politics tended to be judged by where we stood on the question of "armed struggle." The Black Panthers adopted Malcolm X's slogan "by any means necessary." They raised defiant gloved fists in the air. We asked ourselves who would be willing to take up the gun if, as was inevitable, legitimate political processes failed. The Motherfuckers bought shotguns and pistols, cut the shotguns down, and stashed them beneath the floorboards of our apartments. We were preparing for the coming flood of violence and counter violence.

* * *

A great deal of the fantasy of violence that was rife in the movement originated with men. Valerie Solanis was the glorious exception to male rhetorical domination of the language of terror and retribution. She was the founder and sole member of SCUM, the Society for Cutting Up Men. Her *SCUM Manifesto* prophesized:

> SCUM will become members of the unwork force, the fuck-up force. . . . SCUM will forcibly relieve bus drivers, cab drivers and subway token sellers of their jobs and run buses and cabs and dispense free tokens to the public. . . . SCUM will destroy all useless and harmful objects—cars, store windows, "Great Art," etc. . . . Eventually SCUM will take over the airwaves—radio and TV networks—by forcibly relieving of their jobs all radio and TV employees who would impede SCUM's entry into the broadcasting studios. . . . SCUM will couple-bust—barge into mixed (male-female) couples, wherever they are, and bust them up. . . . SCUM will keep on destroying, looting, fucking-up and killing until the money-work system no longer exists and automation is completely instituted or until enough women co-operate with SCUM to make violence unnecessary to achieve these goals, that is, until enough women either unwork or quit work, start looting, leave men and refuse to obey all laws inappropriate to a truly civilized society.

Ben met Valerie one day on the corner of 8th Street and 5th Avenue in the West Village. He was selling *Black Mask* for a nickel a copy. She came up to him and said "I'd like to have one of those, but I don't have a nickel. Ben said that's all right, you can have one. She then went into a bookstore and stole a copy of her manifesto for him. After that they became friends. She sometimes stayed at his loft. She told him he could be part of SCUM's men's auxiliary. "We can't spare you," she said to him, "but we can save you for last."

We never knew when rhetoric would leap the firewall that separated it from reality. During the strike at Columbia University, Valerie climbed through a window in the Mathematics building to ask Ben what would happen if she shot someone. Ben said it would depend on whom she shot and if he died. Less than two months later on, June 3, 1968, she shot Andy Warhol.* As soon as he heard the news Ben cranked out a flier that claimed her as one of us:

> **Andy Warhol Shot by Valerie Solanis. Plastic Man vs. the Sweet Assassin. A tough chick with a bop cap and a .38— the true vengeance of DADA—the 'hater' of men and the lover of 'man'—the camp/master slain by the slave — VALERIE IS OURS.**

Two days later he and Steve traveled uptown and leafleted the Museum of Modern Art. That same day news broke that Robert F. Kennedy had been assassinated.

* * *

In Vietnam, young soldiers, ill prepared for what awaited them, found themselves in a living nightmare that surpassed their wildest fantasies of rape, torture, and death. Back home in the ghetto, Black Panthers were living a dream of killing and

---

* Ben denies the rumor that she got the gun she used from the Motherfuckers as depicted in the 1996 movie, *I Shot Andy Warhol*.

being killed in bloody conflict with the pigs. As the Sixties progressed, we felt compelled to become more "militant." The center was not holding. The freaks of the Lower East Side danced their love dances, swirled their psychedelic garments down the sidewalks, and dreamed acid dreams, while the Motherfuckers teetered towards the realization of the fantasies of Armageddon that filled our flyers. I might hang back just a bit during our violent confrontations with the police, but I could not forever escape the consequences of our rhetoric.

The Atmosphere of the Time Was Ripe with Threats and Prophecies.

CHICAGO AND THE FILLMORE EAST

In the heat of August 1968, television beamed into homes across the United States, images of two Americas clashing on the streets of Chicago. To be more accurate, what viewers saw was one America—the America we called "The System"—beating up on the other America, the America we called "The Movement."

Inside the Convention Center, protected by phalanxes of police and security guards, the Democratic Party recommitted itself to the goal of winning the Vietnam War and nominated Hubert Humphrey to be its presidential candidate. The peace candidacy of Eugene "Clean for Gene" McCarthy shriveled and died. "McCarthy girls," I wrote in the little notebook I carried around with me, "you blond lovelies with silly straw hats and your polka dots, what are you doing in this city bent on blood, what are you doing with your clean pressed collars in this city bent on filth—you with your sorrowful soft faces, what kind of party are you coming to—are you ready for nightmares?"

Humphrey's nomination was all too predictable and stupid. Outside the convention center, on the streets and in the parks, all the strands of the movement—serious SDS activists building a movement to stop the war and imagining a revolution; playful Yippies running a pig for president; Latino and Black youth from the ghettos of Chicago attracted by the spectacle; and long-haired hippies, some dreaming of a street fight, others just dreaming—assembled for, what the Yippies called, a "Festival of Life," to contrast with the "Festival of Death," which was the Democratic Convention.

They camped out in Lincoln Park. The strumming of decal-laden guitars and the wailing of police sirens filled the night. The flames of campfires, the flashbulbs of cameras, and the floodlights of cops cut openings in the darkness. Lines of police emerged from the shadows, adjusting their gas masks and pulling out their billyclubs. We stood for liberation, personal and political, but it was the cops who broke out of all restraints. Night after night they fell upon the protestors with undisguised relish, pushing them from the park.

This was an event made to order for the Motherfuckers. A tight-knit political street gang could have taken the lead in battles with the police. We had an opportunity to demonstrate to a nation-wide audience that neither the idle theorizing of SDS nor the Yippies "it's all fun and games" street theater was an adequate response to the brutal violence the System would unleash if it really felt threatened. The police beat heads and protestors chanted "The whole world is watching." And it was. But it did not see the Motherfuckers.

Ben skipped Chicago altogether. He thought there was already too much police attention on him, and he did not want to lead our following of street kids into danger. He had promised them a safe haven and he meant to keep that promise. So he loaded a bunch of them into a rental car obtained with stolen credit cards and took off across the country. He says he was pursued the entire way by the FBI. He ditched that first car before the heat caught up with him, and continued renting and abandoning rental cars till he reached California, where he drove to the edge of the continent, and pushed the last one over a cliff into the Pacific Ocean. Then he slowly made his way back to New York, stopping along the way in New Mexico.

In Chicago, without Ben and most of the other Mother-fuckers, I felt diminished. I managed—not entirely by accident—to avoid the focal points of confrontation. I stayed just outside of harm's way when the police charged and the billyclubs began to flail, but gave militant speeches in the evening at meetings where we planned the next day's actions. Towards the end of the week, I found myself with thousands of demonstrators penned into Grant Park, with National Guard troops on one side and Chicago police on the other. We were trapped. Our choices were to stay in the park and have an ineffectual rally or attempt to break out of the encir-clement. I was on the stage with Tom Hayden and the other speakers. He gestured to me to come up to the microphone and suggested that I give a speech encouraging the crowd to break through the police lines and take the demonstration to the streets. I gave an appropriately hyperventilating speech, the crowd began to move, and the bloody confrontations con-tinued for another day.

Perhaps because of my speeches, and perhaps because I was the most visible Motherfucker in Chicago, I was named as an unindicted co-conspirator in the indictment that launched the Chicago Conspiracy Trial.

Ben's decision not to go to Chicago represented a turning point for the Motherfuckers. Chicago could have been an opportunity to grow and expand. But we missed it, and remained confined largely to our ghetto. We began a process of withdrawal and shrinking. Ben has since confessed that his decision reflected an internal change, which he kept secret from me at the time. He was beginning to realize that things were not going to change the way we hoped. He was begin-ning to search for a new direction.

* * *

The Motherfuckers were active on the margins of a marginal movement. We did our work and lived our lives in the streets. We didn't keep minutes of meetings and we didn't own a filing cabinet. We churned out ephemeral fliers, but issued no formal press releases. We shunned publicity and our doings went generally unreported in the press. Therefore there are few records with which to correct, order and solidify failing and imperfect memories.

Our battle with Bill Graham is a partial exception. Because he was rock and roll royalty, our confrontation with him was duly noted at the time and has been mentioned in various memoirs since then including *Bill Graham Presents* and *My Life in Rock and Roll* by Bill Graham and Robert Greenfield.

Two months after I returned from Chicago, we initiated a campaign to obtain a free night for the community at the Fillmore East, which Bill Graham, had recently opened on 2nd Avenue as a venue for the rock acts he was promoting. Bill had begun his career managing the San Francisco Mime Troop for almost no money, but now he had become the top rock promoter in the country and was raking in the dough. As we saw it he was making big bucks off our culture and it was time for a little payback. We had a meeting with him to present our demands. The meeting took place in his office behind the theater. It did not go well. Ben's pitch was that suburban kids were coming to the Fillmore in droves to get in on the psychedelic experience, while the kids who lived on the streets of the Lower East Side couldn't afford the price of a ticket. Bill wasn't impressed. The discussion got heated. We made threats and Bill shouted at us that when he was a kid he'd crawled across Europe to escape the Nazis and if he'd survived Hitler, he'd damn well survive us. So that was it. To Bill Graham, born Wolfgang Grajonca, a Jewish orphan born in Berlin, whose mother died in Auschwitz, I had become the equivalent of a Nazi. I tried not to let my distress show, avoided his eyes and concentrated on his watch that had two dials, one set for east coast time, one for west coast time.[18]

The meeting went on for some time. Ben recalls Bill yelling at us that we'd get our free night over his dead body, to which Ben replied with the little smile he got when he was very serious: "Well, that could be arranged." Bill looked him in the eye, opened a drawer of his desk and took out a pair of bullets with chrome casings, which he placed on the desk in front of him. The bullets, he said, were sent to him by the Hell's Angels, who'd once threatened to kill him. He hadn't been scared of them, and he wasn't scared of us. Ben replied that those guys just talked big, but if we decided to shut him down we'd shut him down. Carole remembers things somewhat differently. She says I jumped up and down and yelled, and that it was I who pulled out the bullets and they weren't silver. I don't remember the bullets at all, but Steve remembers it Ben's way. Despite his angry defiance, I had the feeling as we left his office that Bill thrived on confrontation and rather liked us. That was probably wishful thinking.

We continued our campaign. Judith Malina and Julian Beck's Living Theater was scheduled to perform *Paradise Now* at the Fillmore East as part of an evening of radical theater to benefit the legal defense of students arrested at the Columbia University occupation. Ben decided the Living Theater's appearance provided the perfect opportunity to show Bill we meant business. *Paradise Now* was a free form controlled improvisation involving nudity and audience participation. Ben met with Judith and Julian and together they agreed that at the end of the performance the audience would stay and hold the theater. We seeded the audience with contingents of our followers. As the play reached its conclusion, we joined the actors on stage. Richard Goldstein, writing in the *Village Voice*, described what happened next:

> Onstage, 100 people were dancing, chanting or stomping away. Many who knew this scenario by heart were stripping in anticipation. . . . The actors too had bared their bodies; they slipped onstage, formed an even circle, and passed the pipe around. Neighborhood kids moved among the actors, whistling and shouting "Naked City." . . . The performance ended in a huge swirling dance of OM. . . .
>
> At that moment—as though timing were all that was involved—Ben Morea grabbed the microphone and announced on behalf of the Motherfuckers that the Fillmore East had been liberated. He proceeded to demand that Bill Graham turn the house over to "the community" once a week, gratis. Graham's eyes did a soft role in their sockets as he walked into the spotlight to make the confrontation complete.

The performance came to a halt amidst much pandemonium and shouting. Ben announced: "The show is over, life goes on. We're not leaving till we get our one free night." The audience stayed. We drummed and made speeches, some more coherent than others. Much the same argument we had had with Bill in his office now took place in front of an audience. He responded to our demands by saying if we wanted the theater to be free we should buy it, but if we tried to take it by force we would have to kill him first. Finally, well after midnight, Bill took a microphone and announced that if we would leave the theater he would agree to hold a town meeting on our proposal the following Wednesday. We had carried a mimeograph machine to the theater from our office. We brought it on stage and before we left the theater cranked out our cautious response to Bill's offer:

> The community needs free space. It needs to survive, grow freaky, breathe, expand, love, struggle, turn on. Bill Graham, hippie entrepreneur . . . may tonight have been a little liberated or he may not. Next Wednesday will tell. One Nite a Week or the Sky's the Limit.

As it turned out, Bill's idea of what he had offered and ours were not the same.[19]

On the day of the town hall meeting we arrived at the theater and saw on the stage, a table on which sat two microphones. Behind each microphone was a folding chair, one for Bill and one for Ben. Bill wanted a structured debate. He and Ben would talk. The rest of us would listen.

We made sure it wasn't going to happen that way. A Motherfucker event had to include free food, music, spontaneous speeches, call and response. Again we brought a mimeograph machine from our storefront. We set it in the center aisle and, as the event unfolded, churned out fliers commenting on the proceedings. In the face of threats and exhortations from all sides, Bill remained adamantly opposed to giving us our free night. He'd seen what our events looked like and would have none of it. As the night wore on without any discernible progress in the negotiations, people drifted away, and we left, promising to escalate the confrontation.

Behind the scenes, negotiations continued. Other more "responsible" parties, including Wavy Gravy, intervened. Bill finally agreed to allow us to use the theater on Wednesday nights to put on free events for the community.

The first one took place in late November. From our point of view it was an enormous success. The theater was packed.

It felt as if 2nd Avenue had tipped on its side and deposited its entire contents—animate and inanimate—in the theater. Discarded sandwiches, cigarette butts, cans and bottles littered the carpets. Much wine was drunk, much dope was smoked. The program, such as it was, proceeded amidst a chorus of boasts, threats, brags and rambling fantasies shouted out from every corner of the auditorium. Bill Graham's green-shirted ushers stood by, attempting to make themselves inconspicuous, utterly powerless to control the magnificent chaos of the event. The drug laws of the State of New York were flagrantly violated. There were grievous insults to property. Carpets were stained. Seats were broken. Toilets clogged and overflowed.

After four free community nights, and warnings from the police that they would yank his license, Bill Graham had enough. He circulated an open letter to the community announcing the end of the free nights and urging everyone "to *accept our predicament* (which is now *your* reality) with intelligence and grace."

We quickly cranked out a response on our church donated Gestetner:

> Situation: Pigs and Bill Graham stop free night. Why? They say we smoke dope, but we know it's because they are afraid of us. Afraid that we'll learn it's ours. Afraid that we'll get together there to destroy their world and create our own.
>
> The pigs threaten to close Graham down unless he stops our free night. He doesn't have to worry about the pigs. We'll close him down. No free night, no pay night. . . .

On a more conciliatory note we asked to use the theater on the Monday before Christmas for a community meeting to discuss the use of dope. When we showed up the doors were locked.*

Electra records had rented the hall for a free concert the day after Christmas to promote their new acquisition, the MC5, a musically mediocre but politically militant rock and roll band out of Detroit. Its manager, John Sinclair, had been one of the founders of the White Panther Party, a small, Black Panther emulating, anarchist collective, whose rhetoric was a clone of ours. John's White Panther Party Manifesto proclaimed:

> We are a bunch of arrogant motherfuckers and we don't give a damn for any cop or any phony-ass authority control-addict creeps who want to put us down. For the first time in America there is a generation of visionary maniac white motherfucker country dope fiend rock and roll freaks who are ready to get down and kick out the jams—ALL THE JAMS—break everything loose and free everybody from their very real and imaginary prisons—even the chumps and punks and honkies who are always fucking with us.
>
> We demand total freedom for everybody! And we will not be stopped until we get it. We are bad.[20]

The MC5 had played at the last free community night before the shutdown. Radio stations had been giving away free tickets. We demanded 500 tickets for the community. Fearing violence, Graham reluctantly agreed.

---

* Bill's recollection in *Bill Graham Presents* does not jibe with the account given here or with contemporaneous news reports. He claims that we had two months of free nights before he closed us down and then six months passed and then came the night with the Living Theater, which marked the end of our efforts to liberate his theater (Bill Graham and Robert Greenfield, *Bill Graham Presents: My Life in Rock and Roll*, Doubleday, 1992, p. 253–257).

On the evening of the concert the theater filled up quickly and when the doors closed there was still a crowd gathered outside demanding to be let in. The crowd chanted, yelled, and pushed. Bill himself stood in the doorway, blocking the entrance. Suddenly, Israel, one of the Puerto Rican street kids who hung out with us, slashed a bicycle chain across his face. Blood began pouring from his nose. Bill fell back.

The concert began. The MC5 played their big number, 'Kick Out the Jams, Motherfuckers." We gave speeches. The crowd jumped on the stage. Again pandemonium reigned.[21] The band got nervous and made a speedy exit in a limousine, much to our disgust. Wayne Kramer, a member of the MC5 remembers:

> The stage wings were crowded with Motherfuckers waiting for us to give the word to burn the place down. Of course we weren't about to give any such command and their anger started to turn on us. . . . We finished our set and escaped to the dressing room while the motherfuckers and the street maniacs tried to run out the door with our gear. Our crew valiantly battled to hold on to our stuff and the greatest blunder in record business tactics imaginable happens: two limousines show up to carry the band back to the hotel. The revolutionaries saw red! "Limos!" The symbol of capitalist imperial-ism. Limos. The Moth-erfucker women were screaming and weeping about how we had sold the revolution out. They were smashing our records against the Cadillac limos tail fins. Crying at the top of their lungs: "Bastards! Pigs! Phonies! Sell-outs!"[22]

After the MC 5 left, the crowd stayed. Before the night was over one person had been hospitalized after being hit over the head with a microphone stand; a Puerto Rican boy had been stabbed; and one of the ushers had his arm fractured with a metal pipe.[23]

That night marked the end of our battle with Bill Graham. Bill offered to provide some financial and other support for the community to find some other place to meet, but it never happened. Times were changing and the very brief heyday of the Motherfuckers was nearing its end. I had watched Bill get hit with the chain and felt a door open between our violent rhetoric and reality. I did not want to walk through it. The vulnerability of the flesh of my opponent gave me no pleasure.

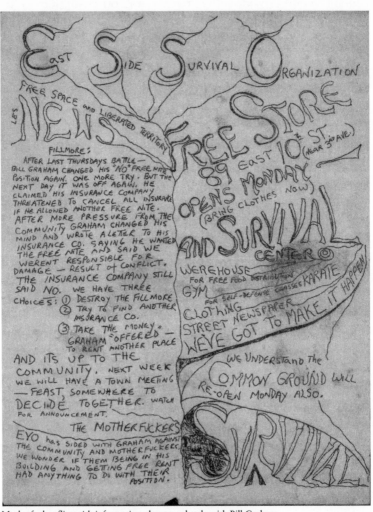

Motherfucker flier with information about our battle with Bill Graham.

ENDGAME

By 1969, it was becoming clear that the cultural weather was changing. The season of love, rage, and extravagant expectations was coming to an end. On the streets of the Lower East Side, hard drugs began to replace LSD. The young dropouts had a nervous jagged edge. We had opened up our free store as a nighttime crashpad. It would fill with drunks who'd wake in the middle of the night, and go after each other with broken wine bottles. Optimism was giving way to a tight-lipped struggle for survival. The emotional tone of the Motherfuckers darkened. Our stash of guns was a source of endless paranoia. We were constantly moving it from one hiding place to another.

Some months after the last of our Fillmore East nights, Ben was standing with his girlfriend, Joan, on the corner of 10th Street and 3rd Avenue when a car pulled up across the street with three men in it. A heavyset guy got out, walked over to Ben and said: "We've been hired to kill you." Joan ran off towards Gem's Spa two blocks away to get help and soon returned with ten to fifteen people. Ben said to the guys in the car: "If you try to kill me you better make sure I die." They drove off.

At the end of one of our numerous confrontations with the police on St. Marks Place, I was arrested and taken to the Ninth precinct. I was handcuffed with my hands behind my back to a chair in the middle of the squad room. The room was full of officers from the Tactical Patrol Force. The cops dragged in a young street kid. He was thin and frail, had long black hair, and was wearing a shirt that had been made from an American flag. The cops gathered around him. They didn't say a word. In the corner of the room was a machine for polishing shoes. It had wheel with bristles at floor level, which spun when the switch was turned on. One of the cops led the boy over to the machine, pressed his face against the wheel and pushed the switch. It lasted for only a moment or two. The boy didn't make a sound. I was too afraid to protest. When it was over a cop came over and casually slapped me a couple of times in the face. I had a sinking feeling that my whole world of fantasized violence was about to descend on me in earnest. But the moment passed.

I was not the only one who was emotionally unprepared for real violence. Charlie always endeavored to be the perfect Motherfucker, despite a gentle and introspective nature. He was fiercely loyal to Ben. In 1961 he had participated in the Freedom Rides organized by CORE. When he came back he had drifted away from politics, and found work as a market researcher. He took to wearing cashmere coats and a beret. His conversion experience came when he met Ben at Back Mask's "Change Wall Street to War Street" demonstration. In short order he ditched his cashmere coat for a black leather jacket, grew a full beard and moved in with the Motherfuckers, accompanied by Carole and her new born baby Chacha.

Carole and Charlie had met in an earlier life when they were both acting in amateur Comedia del Arte productions. Carole had been going to college, living with a man considerably older than herself, and waitressing at a Middle Eastern Restaurant in Greenwich Village. It took one very good LSD trip to change her from a "regular person" wearing skirts and blouses to a hippie who wrapped herself in the curtains from her apartment. In quick succession she quit her job, dropped out of college, moved to Timothy Leary's ashram at Millbrook, got pregnant, moved back to New York, and delivered Cha Cha by Cesarean section in the maternity ward of a public hospital. She had lost track of Charlie, but as she was staggering back from the hospital, carrying her baby in her arms, holding herself up by the buildings, Charlie happened to pass by in a beat up pickup truck he was using to collect food for a free Motherfucker community feed. Charlie and Carole got back together and moved into an apartment with Alfonso and Alan on Avenue B.

Charlie and Carole were the perfect Motherfucker couple. When a cop politely suggested Carole could find a more private place to breast-feed than the corner of 2nd Avenue and St. Marks Place, she whipped out her tit and squirted him full in the chest with breast milk. And Charlie was always ready at Ben's side, to prove himself and do what needed to be done.

It was therefore not surprising that during one of our demonstrations, in which we had taken over St. Marks Place, and filled the street with demonstrators blowing penny whistles, it was Charlie who came to the rescue of little Caesar, one of our entourage of Puerto Rican street kids, when the police grabbed him and attempted to drag him into a patrol car. Charlie ran over, surprised the cops who were holding Caesar, and pulled him loose. Caesar escaped but Charlie was not so lucky. Within seconds the police grabbed him and hustled him into Gem's Spa. Through the window we could see him being dragged to the back of the store. Ben was as fiercely loyal to Charlie as Charlie was to him. When he saw the police dragging Charlie away he charged through the crowd and kicked in the window of the store. Charlie broke away from the police and jumped through the broken window, but was immediately recaptured. The cops were enraged. They called in reinforcements, marched Charlie into a paddy wagon, and took him to the precinct station.

Charlie never talked to me about what happened there, but he told Carole that he was taken into a back room by cops who were members of the Tactical Patrol Force. One of them took the lead, beating him with a shoe and then a nightstick. One blow fractured his arm and another his skull. The beating Charlie took in that room did something terrible to the core of his being from which he never completely recovered. It was as if the police had reamed him out and filled the emptiness they created with fear. They took away his words. He stopped speaking.

Carole was away in California when the incident happened. When the news reached her, she hurried back to New York and began looking for Charlie. Nobody seemed to know where he was. Finally she discovered him in Alfonso Motherfucker's apartment, sitting in the bathtub with his broken arm in a cast. He was almost catatonic. He hadn't eaten. He couldn't walk. He couldn't get into bed by himself. He was broken in body and spirit.

When he was somewhat recovered, Charlie took to spending his days with Caesar, sneaking into women's apartments to steal money and candy. He still didn't talk. Once when Carole caught him looking through someone's apartment, he tied her up in a stairwell and left her for two hours. He couldn't explain why. She determined she had to get him out of New York and away from the Motherfuckers. Ben accused her of betraying the revolution and breaking up the group. She told him she didn't care. She panhandled for two days to get enough money to get out of New York. She and Charlie caught a ride heading west. They drove across the George Washington Bridge, and when they had crossed the Hudson and reached New Jersey, Charlie turned to her and said "So, it's a pretty nice day, today, isn't it." Those were the first words he'd spoken in a month.

That's Carole's recollection. I have a slightly different memory of Charlie after his beating. I remember a Charlie who regained his speech, but whose thoughts seemed to drift about like boats cut loose from their anchors, a Charlie who spoke in a soft monotone, as if he had wondered a great distance off and was talking to himself. I remember his voice as an echo in an empty shell. But perhaps Carole is right and the Charlie I remember is the Charlie before the beating, a Charlie who was already a little far away, an echoing shell but not a broken one.

* * *

We seemed to be attracting craziness. I felt the balance in the group tip. Some of the older original Motherfuckers drifted away. New recruits were often tough guys from the street, drawn by our rhetoric of violence. Ben felt the need to augment the Motherfuckers with some real muscle. He brought in Barry Motherfucker, who, like Ben, had been a heroin addict, but unlike Ben, was still a user. Barry was a wise cracking Jewish gangster from Brooklyn. His father was rumored to be a powerful lawyer or a judge. I never understood what drew Barry to the Motherfuckers. Perhaps it was, as Steve remembers, that he adored Ben. Whatever it was, it didn't seem to be our politics.

I was wary of Barry from the beginning and so were some of the other original Motherfuckers. Alfonso Motherfucker was a soft-spoken Puerto Rican poet with legs crippled by polio. He had been expelled from the University of Puerto Rico for his involvement in the Puerto Rican Independence

Movement. Alfonso remembers walking down Haight Street with Barry during a trip to California in 1970. Suddenly, and without warning, Barry walked up to a Black man who was making a phone call from a phone booth, stuck his fingers in the man's side imitating a gun, and took his wallet. Alfonso walked away vowing never to associate with Barry again.*

* * *

It's no wonder that Ben was looking around for soldiers. Being a shrewd judge of character, he surely realized I would not be much use in combat. The truth is that I never learned to fight and I was terrified of violence. I generally managed to skirt danger, but when it was absolutely unavoidable, I can only describe my behavior as cowardly.

I remember one incident in which I became literally paralyzed by fear. We had traveled to Boston, at the request of a group of street kids who hung out on Boston Common, a seventy-five acre park in the center of the city. They had been attacked by gangs of off-duty service men and constantly harassed by the police. We held a rally to support them, and defying a nighttime curfew, stayed with them till the morning. The next day the police massed and drove us from the park. We regrouped at Arlington church at the foot of the Common for a meeting. The meeting was to take place in the basement. When we arrived, many of the kids who had been in the park had already gone inside. Suddenly cars drove up and about twenty drunken marines got out, opened the trunks, and pulled out baseball bats. A fight ensued. We drew our little knives, and all around the parking lot we were dodging bats and stabbing with our knives. I cowered inglo-

---

* Not everyone shared Alfonso's and my wariness of Barry. Jonathan, one of the younger Motherfuckers, still remembers him with affection. Jonathan says Barry had a great tough-guy sense of humor, was always kind to him, and treated him like a little brother.

riously on the sideline. When the police arrived Ben was still defending himself. He'd been backed into a corner and two marines were swinging at him. Those of us who could scattered and reassembled in an apartment where we had been staying. We were freaked out. Some of us had been hit by bats. Alan complained about a knife wound he had suffered. He sat on the toilet moaning.

Ben was not able to escape. The cops arrested him and cuffed him, but never found his knife, which he managed to conceal in his fist and jam down a crack in the back seat of the patrol car that took him to jail. In the course of the fight, one of the marines had been stabbed. He was wounded so severely he almost died. Although he had not done it, the cops accused Ben of the stabbing.

He was charged with attempted murder, and faced a possible sentence of twenty-five years. The charge was later reduced to assault. At the trial, Ben's lawyer urged him not to take the stand. He did anyway, long hair and all, dressed in a suit, with beads around his neck. He was an excellent witness. His defense was that he hadn't stabbed the marine, but if he had, it would have been justifiable self-defense. The jurors went into the jury room to deliberate. It didn't look good. The Vietnam War was raging. Ben was accused of attempting to kill one of "our boys." Initially eleven jurors were for conviction. The one hold out was the only African American on the panel. He managed to persuade the other jurors there was reasonable doubt. Ben was acquitted.

* * *

In the rhetoric of the movement, the bourgeois values of America masked its barbarism. But for me, the relation between mask and reality was reversed. My barbaric Motherfucker exterior masked my ambivalent relation to bourgeois values. I hid my fear, my insecurity, and my obsessions beneath a façade of bravado. My strategy for self-preservation was to maintain the split between my hidden private world and my public persona that I had hoped to overcome by immersion in radical politics.

As a dirty Motherfucker, I acted out with enthusiasm my disdain for decorum and convention. But despite my posturing, I remained plagued by sadomasochistic fantasies and an obsession with my own filthiness—my pores, pimples, and smells. Perhaps because of these obsessions, I raged with a special vehemence, like a prisoner frantically struggling to free himself of his shackles.

The System was shit. Not I. Or rather, if I was shit, then I would be shit with a vengeance. I reveled in the power of excrement. I would reduce "the System" to garbage. I would clamber over it like a rat in a dump. I, who felt like shit, hurled shit at my enemies.[24] "You are shit" I screamed, at professors, generals, judges, and banqueters emerging from their limousines. "Fuck the war." "Fuck Johnson." "Fuck all you pompous asses." Treating "no-trespass" signs as invitations, shoplifting from supermarkets, turning over garbage cans, hurling muck and rocks and invective, I became a human dirt ball. I ignored stoplights. I preferred running in the street to walking on the sidewalk. The sound of breaking glass was music to my ears.

And still I worried about pimples.

At about the same time that I was beginning my involvement with the Motherfuckers, I began a relationship with Yeshi, whom I would later marry and who would become the mother of my children. Yeshi had taught at Tuskegee Institute in Tuskegee, Alabama and participated in the march from Selma to Montgomery. When we first got together she was working as an organizer at Mobilization for Youth, an anti-poverty agency on the Lower East Side funded through Lyndon Johnson's War on Poverty. Her job was to help Puerto Rican women on welfare set up sewing cooperatives. In her Frye boots and blue suede mini-skirt she looked to me the very embodiment of radical chic. And she had a living space to match her outfits: a nice apartment in a building with an elevator, overlooking a quiet churchyard on 10th Street and 2nd Avenue.

Until now, my relations with women had consisted of my time with Prudence in London, a few brooding, guilt-ridden, sexually dysfunctional affairs, and one spectacular experience of anonymous sex. With Yeshi I had the possibility of an intimate sexual relation that could serve as an antidote to my sadomasochistic fantasy life. I took refuge in her embrace— from the street, from our constant confrontations, threats, counter-threats, and from my fantasies. Yeshi steered clear of the Motherfuckers as much as possible. She felt scorned by them as a useless bourgeois woman. I would lie with her in bed, worrying that I was missing something out on St. Marks Place, but sure that I needed to be "cured" of my introversion by a real relation to a woman.

In the street, I played the role of cultural terrorist, prophet of instinctual release, vengeful and relentless. I'd return from raging in the streets, to find myself impotent in bed. Yeshi would lie with me, coaxing sexuality out of me, quieting me, and gently ridiculing my fears. I handed out flyers filled with inflamed rhetoric, taunted the police, proclaimed the liberation of fantasy, but ran from that fantasy into the arms of a woman. Once safe, I immediately feared that my refuge would become a prison. Yeshi would be my Delilah, ready with her shears to trim my fury. She would turn me into a timid, trapped plaything. She would isolate me in some cute little Greenwich Village apartment where she and I would sit at the kitchen table, dipping pieces of croissant into our coffee cups, and on Sundays, languidly turning the pages of the *New York Times*. Oh the shame of it!

As it turned out, I didn't have to worry about the consequences of a cozy private life with Yeshi. The neat compartments into which I had divided my life collapsed dramatically after a fire destroyed two Motherfucker crash pads on 4th Street. Ben's dog and Johnny's cat died in the blaze. After the fire, the newly homeless Motherfuckers invaded Yeshi's apartment. My comrades tore down her Picasso prints and spray painted "Down with the Bourgeoisie" on the walls of her living room. She and I would come home to find Motherfuckers sleeping in our bed.

Day after day, Motherfuckers would ride up and down in the narrow elevator, watched disapprovingly by the Puerto Rican superintendent. He became increasingly upset about the invasion of his building. Israel, one of the Puerto Rican street kids who attached themselves to us, spray-painted graffiti in the halls. Every time the super cleaned it off, Israel would do it again.

One evening, Joan, Israel, and Jamie, another of our Puerto Rican street kids, had been hanging out together. When they came back home and entered the downstairs lobby they noticed the superintendent staring at them. Joan doesn't remember anything being said, but the expression on his face frightened her. She pushed the button for the elevator. When it opened they hurried in. But they were not quick enough. The superintendent had armed himself with a bottle of acid. He rushed towards them, hurled the acid, and hit Jamie full in the face. Jamie was taken to the hospital. He wore the scars for the rest of his short life and was never mentally the same.

Hours after the incident Jamie's friends were in our apartment. They looked out the window, and there was the superintendent, sitting on a lawn chair outside the building, having a beer as if nothing had happened. Everyone went berserk. They rushed downstairs. Someone stabbed him with a knife. He died.

We shouted "Off the pig," but the first person we killed was a Puerto Rican superintendent. The killing never made the papers. My questions about what happened were met with impatience. I did not need to know what happened. All I needed to know was that he had to die. You can not live on the streets and allow yourself to be attacked without defending yourself.

About the time the Motherfuckers were turning Yeshi's apartment into their crash pad, a biker gang set up their headquarters in a loft on 3rd Street. Now there were two gangs on the Lower East Side, the Motherfuckers and the Gypsy Jokers. One day two of the Jokers showed up at Yeshi's apartment looking for Barry. Ben let them in. They said that Barry had ratted one of them out in a dope deal. They had a contract out on him and they were going to kill him. He had a choice. They could kill him there in the apartment or he could come with them and they'd kill him somewhere else. Ben had a 25-caliber pistol in his pocket. He said to them, "I don't know what's going on, but you're not going to kill him, not here or anywhere, because if you try, one of you is going to die." They left. They told Ben the hit had been ordered by their leader. Ben went to their headquarters and confronted him. He was a head taller than Ben. They both pulled knives and began to circle each other from one end of the loft to the other, talking all the while. In the end they put away their knives and shook hands.

Peace was restored, but it didn't last long. Another biker gang, the Aliens, who later affiliated with the Hells Angels, moved into town and went to war with the Gypsy Jokers. The war ended when the Aliens raided the Gypsy Jokers' headquarters. They tied the leader of the Jokers to a chair and set the loft on fire. He burned to death. Not long afterwards the police raided Ben's apartment on Mott Street and found a stash of guns, acid, and explosives, and a roster book containing the names and badge numbers of members of the Tactical Patrol Force.

We continued to swagger, but the circle was closing in on us. I was not the only one who felt it. Charlie was gone. Other Motherfuckers drifted away. Ben had made up his mind to change course. We had mined a thin vein. It was giving out. We were deep underground, unsure of the supports shoring up the mineshaft. The little canary that warns when the air becomes unbreathable was beginning to cough and wheeze. It was time to get out.

NEW MEXICO

Ben had heard about a hippie gathering of the tribes that was to take place in New Mexico and decided the time had come for us to make our escape from the ghetto. He was determined not to abandon the rainbow of kids who hung out with us and told them that if they wanted to come with us, we'd find room for them. He scored an old school bus from Saul Gottlieb of the Living Theater. But he didn't have money for gas or supplies. He was trying to figure out what to do when he ran into Paul Krassner outside the Odessa Restaurant and pitched him the plight of the kids. Krassner told him to wait. He'd be right back. He walked away and in a short while came back with a check for three thousand dollars. Armed with a working vehicle and gas money, the Motherfuckers packed their bags and set out across the country, shoplifting along the way. Yeshi and I drove out separately.

In the late Sixties, hippies were moving into the Mexican villages of New Mexico as earlier they had moved into the Puerto Rican tenements of the Lower East Side. Ben had no intention of joining one of the blissed-out hippie communes proliferating in the dry windswept plains around Taos. He had something quite different in mind. He arranged a meeting with Elizabeth Sutherland (now Betita Martinez) who lived in Española, where she edited *El Grito Del Norte*, a newspaper that served as the mouthpiece of the Alianza, a militant Chicano movement for land rights. The goal of the Alianza was to reclaim ownership of the original Spanish and Mexican land grants that had been incorporated into the National Forest. The movement's founder, Reis Tijerina, hoped to spark an armed insurrection by leading a series of raids on government institutions. On June 6, 1967, Tijerina and a group of his men stormed the courthouse in Tierra Amarilla, the county seat a few miles north of Canjilón. They freed prisoners, shot a policeman and a jailer, and fled with a reporter and deputy sheriff as hostages.

Through Elizabeth we met two brothers, Juan and Tony, who had been lieutenants in Tijerina's little army and leaders in the courthouse raid. They lived in Canjilón, a tiny mountain village about sixty miles up the road from Española and forty miles south of the Colorado border. Canjilón was an Alianza stronghold. During the manhunt that followed the courthouse raid, the National Guard occupied Canjilón. The men of the town hid in the hills during the day, and snuck back at night for dinner. Eventually Tijerina was captured. By the time we arrived he had been tried, convicted, and sentenced to prison. The men of Canjilón returned to eking out a living surrounded by National Forest they considered stolen from them by the US government. They were not reconciled. They awaited the time when they would rise again. Juan saw us as potentially valuable allies. He knew we had guns and they would need all the guns they could get. He agreed to let us live rent-free in a little three-room adobe house he owned in the village. Ben told Juan we'd be ready when we were needed. This clearly was the place for us.

But we were city kids. We had little idea what to do with ourselves in the country. We had no way to earn a living even if we had wanted to. We drove down the road to Española, signed up for food stamps, bought guns, and went off to hunt

deer in the national forest. We started a compost pile and a
garden, and dug an outhouse. We acquired a couple of goats,
a few chickens, a rooster, a stray dog with distemper who ate
the rooster, a flat bed truck, and a VW bus with eyes painted
on the side. We used the truck to steal hay to feed our two
goats. Once we rustled a cow. It was standing alone in an
empty field when we drove by. We shot it, wrestled it into our
VW bus, drove to a place we would not be observed and
skinned it with a knife. The knife was dull. It took forever. We
got it home, ate cow till we couldn't eat anymore, then gave
the rest away. Because we had read that Native Americans
used every part of the animals they killed, we decided to tan
the skin and make a drum. Two methods of tanning were pro-
posed: stewing in birch bark and stewing in urine. We
compromised and combined the two methods. We submerged
the skin in a barrel with the mixture. The barrel stank. The
skin marinated. When we examined it two weeks later, it had
turned to jelly. We intended to make the body of the drum
from a log, which we would hollow out by burning out its
center with coals from the fire. This method required constant
careful attention. Whoever was overseeing the task neglected
his duties. The coals burnt big holes in the sides and the log
broke into pieces.

We read *Black Elk Speaks*, which purported to be the
reflections of an Oglala Sioux medicine man.[25] Black Elk
thought it was a bad idea to live in square houses. We decided
to build an underground kiva in our backyard. We dug a long
oval hole, carefully leveling the floor and smoothing out the
sides. With the mud we dug out of the hole we made adobe
bricks and constructed a domed roof. It had a smoke hole at
one end. On winter solstice we built a fire and took peyote.
We sat in a circle, chanting while the smoke curled out the
smoke hole and up into the cold crystal moonlit night. Unfor-

tunately, almost as soon as we finished construction, the kiva began to collapse. We had built it too close to an irrigation ditch. The water from the ditch seeped through the walls, and our beautiful domed roof collapsed in a pile of rubble.

Isolated in our little home in the country we read about the formation of the Weathermen, about their Days of Rage, and how they put on helmets and fought the Chicago police. We read about the explosion in the Greenwich Village town house that killed three of their members who had been trying to manufacture a bomb. The Weathermen were the new Motherfuckers. A visitor passing through Canjilón reported that I'd been named a co-conspirator in the indictment that preceded the Chicago 7 conspiracy trial. It all seemed very far away. On July 20, 1969, "Buzz" Aldrin walked on the Sea of Tranquility. A few months later, we sat out on a mesa surrounded by stars and looked up at the moon. Its light poured down on us and I wondered how we had become so marginalized.

Isolated, no longer able to imagine ourselves at the center of history, the remnants of the Motherfuckers began to turn on each other. Ben's tyrannical nature became ever more intolerable. Craziness seemed to spread through the ranks. One day I was at the wheel of our old VW bus, driving down the mountain road that winds from Canjilón to Española and enjoying the view of the yellow ochre sandstone bluffs that Georgia O'Keefe loved to paint, when suddenly I lost control going around a curve. The bus rolled over and skidded towards the cliff. I remember looking out the window and seeing Alfonso Motherfucker, who had been thrown out the sliding side door, flying in the air above the bus, withered leg and all, like a figure in a Chagall painting.* The bus came to a stop just short of the edge. Miraculously no one was hurt.

---

* Alfonso remembers it differently. He believes he stayed in the bus, and recalls seeing the spare tire rolling around inside. I prefer my memory.

We stashed the guns we were carrying in the brush in case the police came by and waited for someone to stop and offer help.

Our presence in Canjilón did not go unnoticed by the authorities. The police started cruising by our house on a regular basis. One day I was working on a truck out on the road in front of our house when a police car stopped and two sheriffs got out. My hands were covered in grease. My hair hung down below my shoulders. Without explanation or excuse, they ordered me to stand up and put down my tools. Then they searched me, handcuffed me, and hustled me into their patrol car. They drove me to their little one room station house and locked me in a holding cell. I gave a false name and spent the next hours rubbing my fingertips against the cement wall in an effort to erase my fingerprints. After some time they took me out of the cell, took my photograph and fingerprints, and then locked me back up. Hours later, they ushered me out of my cell, handed me my back my wallet and my shoes, and let me go.

Ben maintained a good relationship with Juan and Tony. They took him out hunting for deer and elk and on occasion he joined them on an expedition to round up the wild horses that roamed in the high meadows of the national forest. We helped haphazardly when it was time to bring in the hay, but by and large we lived apart from the townspeople, with whom we had very little communication. One evening as we were lounging outside our house, we heard little explosions in the distance. Something wushed by our heads. It took me a moment to realize that someone was shooting at us. The shots seemed to come from the direction of a clump of houses at the other side of a field. We ran and got our guns and fired back in the general direction of the houses from which the shots had come. I took the incident as a sign that we were no longer welcome, but Juan reassured Ben that we had just gotten caught in an argument between him and people in the village who didn't like him. Despite his assurances, we were part of the problem. The argument had a political dimension. Not everyone in Canjilón was prepared to plot another insurrection, nor happy with Juan's choice of hippy weirdoes as comrades in arms.

Even I, most committed of Motherfuckers, was beginning to realize that Canjilón was a dead end. Yeshi had given up her job at Mobilization for Youth to come with me to New Mexico. Her patience with the Motherfuckers, close to non-existent to begin with, wore out long before mine did. She and Ben's partner, Joan, cooked for the men. There was no running hot water. After six months in New Mexico she developed a bad case of hepatitis and left to recover with her sister in La Jolla. I visited her. We made love. She conceived our first child. I returned to New Mexico. She wrote me telling me she was pregnant, and announced she was not returning to the Motherfuckers. I could stay with them or I could go with her. I couldn't do both. I chose the mother over the fuckers. We packed the red VW bus she had borrowed from her sister and I left the Motherfuckers for good. It felt like I was stepping off the edge of the earth.

Not long after we left, the Motherfuckers pulled up stakes and moved out of Canjilón. The group was beginning to dwindle away. Ben was spending more and more time in the mountains, hunting, gathering, and learning how to survive in the woods. For the time being he was done living in square houses. He planned to caravan with the remaining Motherfuckers around Northern New Mexico, buy or trade for horses, and then take off into the National Forest to see if he could survive off the land.

Death was not done stalking the Motherfuckers. Ritchie had been with the Motherfuckers on and off since the Columbia University strike. He had joined the small band that followed Ben into the mountains. He left after Ben and he had an argument over his shooting of a rabbit with a high-powered rifle at a time when Ben was trying to travel without attracting notice. A few months after he left, Ritchie fell and injured his leg. He was living in a cabin with a woman, Lyric, and they'd had kids together. The wound wouldn't heal, and he wouldn't go to the hospital. He watched it turn purple and ugly, and did nothing while a red line worked its way up his leg. By the time he finally went to the clinic in Mora it was too late. He died of septicemia.

Barry left the Motherfuckers to form his own small band of armed banditos. Ben tried to get Barry to stay with him, but he refused. The lure of the thug life was too great. Within months Barry was shot to death trying to rip off a dope deal in Albuquerque.

A Sicilian kid from New York who went by the name Sunshine hooked up with the remnants of the Motherfuckers after Ben left Canjilón. Sunshine rode with Ben for a while and changed his name to Lobo. After a while he decided to break away and form his own band of armed banditos. They rode into El Rio and got into a gunfight with state police. Lobo was shot in the leg, but managed to escape. Later he was killed by members of his own gang.

There were by now too many men with guns and horses living in the mountains to avoid the attentions of the authorities. Ben decided to leave northern New Mexico and head for Colorado.

As Ben headed off to Colorado and those who remained behind began dying, Yeshi and I drove around Northern New Mexico, looking for a place to have a baby. We stayed for a few months in a cabin in a mountain valley outside of Mora on the eastern slopes of the Sangre De Cristo mountains. I have never lived in a more beautiful place. From our front door we could look out over the valley and see the silver strands of waterfalls, plunging off the edge of the snowcapped peaks surrounding the Pecos wilderness. We shared the valley with an old couple who kept goats. They had a dog whose job it was to herd the goats, which she did with wonderful skill and enthusiasm.

One day Yeshi and I jumped naked into an ice-cold mountain lake, scrambled out onto the bank and declared ourselves married. We would have been happy to stay in our valley, but winter was coming on and we would have been snowed in when the baby was due. We packed up and headed for California. On the last day of 1970 in Berkeley, California, my first daughter was born at home in a little cottage on Regent Street on a bed covered with a blue blanket on which Yeshi had embroidered a red eagle. We named her Rainbow, a perfect hippy name she promptly discarded in favor of Rachel when she hit high school, having grown tired of all the rainbow-themed presents with which she'd be inundated on her birthdays.

AFTER THE REVOLUTION THAT DIDN'T HAPPEN, LIFE GOES ON

For a while after Rachel's birth, Yeshi and I prolonged our countercultural existence at Black Bear Ranch, a rural commune in Northern California, set high in a mountain valley an hour's drive by logging road from the wild rock-sculpting, fish spawning, Salmon River. We were snowed-in in the winter. We had no telephone. We generated all our electricity with Pelton wheels driven by water we channeled from the creeks that ran through the property.

Black Bear had once been a thriving mining community. Black Bear Mine, abandoned by the time we arrived, had been one of the most profitable gold mines in California. Our Main House was a rambling two-story wood-frame building, which had been the home of the mine owner, John Daggett, who made his fortune mining and subsequently rose to become Lt. Governor of California. Our wood shop had been the community's post office.

The entire first floor of our Main House was one big L shaped room. At one end was the kitchen where we cooked on a huge cast-iron wood-burning stove. In the rest of the room we ate together at a long wooden table, hung out, held meetings, and played music in the evenings. We all chopped wood, cared for the children, learned to fix our trucks and run our chain saws. In the mornings and evenings we milked our herd of goats. We earned a little money planting trees in clearcuts for the Forest Service, and fighting forest fires. All the money we earned went into a collective pot.

We slept together in communal houses and experimented with non-monogamy. In the summer we ran around naked. We had first hand knowledge of each other's breasts and butts, penises and pubic hairs. We peed wherever we happened to be. I was very good at peeing while walking down the road. Women squatted wherever the urge came over them, and piss would stream in little rivulets out between their legs.

The goats had the run of the land. We fenced in the gardens to keep them out and let them graze. They shat black fibrous pellets that came out like licorice gumballs from a penny gum machine. We, the humans shat side by side in a hexagonal shitter we built above the Main House. It had smoothly sanded holes, and wooden lids with which to cover the holes when you were done. We shat together in the heat of summer and the cold of winter, shat evening shits after dinner, and morning shits after breakfast. We shat with the children sitting on the smaller kids' shitter holes looking up at us, their eyes large and inscrutable like the eyes of animals while our turds fell with a soft thud onto a peeked, somehow comforting mound below, mixed in with paper and topped with a sprinkle of white lime.

Our bodies excreted next to other bodies similarly excreting, some easily, some straining, doing it together in a kind of communal privacy emblematic of our mode of conducting the intercourse between our public and private lives. We shared shitting as we shared the sounds of fucking in the night, and the glimpses of humping bodies by the light of a kerosene lamp. We knew each other in an extended intimacy I have never encountered at any other time or place. Gradually, I unbuckled the emotional armor I had learned to wear around men during the Motherfucker days.

For me it was basically all good. I almost learned to love my body. One afternoon I was shoveling hot rocks with a rusty shovel through an opening in a dome of rotting plastic that we used for a steam bath. The rocks glowed red from the fire and were covered with white ash. I was naked. I was enjoying the shoveling. And suddenly I became aware that I felt strong and that my muscles worked well. I realized I liked my naked body and the feel of the air caressing my bare skin and the heat of the fire. I had never imagined as a child or a Motherfucker, that I would have such a body or would feel this good about it.

I loved the communal life. I loved the fucking. We were freeing ourselves, I thought, from the rigid structuring of intimate relations. Relationships didn't need to be exclusive. Couples did not have to surround themselves with a zone of privacy. Women have told me since then that they did not always enjoy the evening mating dance, wondering who would go off into the night with whom, and who would be left hanging around the Main House. For many of them, all that non-exclusive fucking (Was it good for you? Did you come? Men never seem to know) was not such a great experience. I thought at the time that our efforts to take communal responsibility for the children were wonderful for the children, who were freed from dependence on one or two parents, who might or might not be available. And it was for some of them. But I know now that some of the children felt lied to and abandoned, and didn't believe us when we said "we're all your mothers and fathers." Others were afraid of some of the men.

For all our diversity of body types, we were mainly white. My best friend Sabi, who was part Puerto Rican and part Dominican and who grew up in Harlem, had no nostalgia for Black Bear. He arrived at the ranch with his four children and worried about the future, because he knew that for all our protestations of community it wouldn't last forever. The white people would go off to claim their privilege, and he'd be left fending for himself.

We who lived at Black Bear remain an extended family, but we no longer, if we ever really did, share the wealth. Some of us have remained close. Others of us have drifted apart. Some of us are making good money. Some of us are just getting by. I treasure my memories: of being naked to each other, of intimate exposure, of a wonderful collective privacy, of a time when we had the expectation that we would take from the common pot what we needed, and pour into it what we could.

* * *

After a couple of years living at Black Bear, I grew dissatisfied with our isolation from the world, and decided to return to the city. Yeshi and Rachel accompanied me. Yeshi went to nursing school. I took up mural painting, inspired to return to making art by the murals I had seen in the Mission district of San Francisco. We had another child, Emma. And then, when Emma was two years old, we divorced. I initiated the break-up because . . . well, the usual becauses—a feeling of being trapped, a building up of resentments. "Happy families are all alike; every unhappy family is unhappy in its own way," is the famous first line of the first chapter of Tolstoy's Anna Karenina, but I'm not sure it's true. I think unhappiness can be far more banal and generic than happiness. I sat in the car outside our home the evening I left, looked up at the lighted windows, already terribly missing my children, and cried uncontrollably. Banal or not, it hurt.

Within a year after leaving Yeshi, I moved in with Anna. She and I had been working together on the board of a community arts organization. She was a ceramic artist and singer, and was active in Berkeley politics. I imagined she could be my perfect partner, a warrior for justice, a comrade in arms. It didn't work out that way. The relationship gradually deteriorated and turned into a nightmare from which Rachel and Emma, who shuttled back and forth between our house and Yeshi's, longed to escape.

I left Anna after eight years. Before I'd moved in with her, I'd been occasional lovers with Arisika. When Anna found out she went ballistic. Arisika and I stopped seeing each other altogether. Leaving Anna enabled me to reconnect with Ariska. We discovered we still liked each other. We married in 1993, and have lived together ever since.

* * *

In 1982 I helped organize massive demonstrations against nuclear weapons research at the Lawrence Livermore Laboratories. Over a thousand people were arrested at various times. I spent two and a half weeks in jail with hundreds of other protestors. On one occasion the county jail ran out of room and had to house us in giant circus tents. I was sitting in jail when we heard the news of the massacres of Palestinians in the Lebanese refugee camps at Sabra and Chatilla. The week we got out, a group of us who were Jewish went to the Israeli consulate and got ourselves arrested for blocking the entranceway. In 1985 I participated in anti-apartheid demonstrations at the University of California and was arrested on the steps of Sproul Hall and in front of the chancellor's office where a shantytown had been built. I'd started law school the year before. I didn't see how I could make a living painting political murals and doubted my talent. I studied for the bar exam while sitting in a holding tank in the basement of the

Federal building after I was arrested for protesting the war in El Salvador. While still in law school, a friend of mine and I decided that when we graduated and got our bar cards, we'd rent a stall in the Berkeley Flea market and offer consults alongside the vendors of pots and pans and secondhand clothing. I was still with Anna. She and some other lawyers joined us. We called ourselves Fleagal Aid. We set up our pin-striped tent, and for a while dispensed the cheapest, and hopefully not the worst, legal advice in town.

For eight years, from 1984 to 1992, I sat on Berkeley's Civilian Police Review Commission. The cops hated me. In 1987 I was diagnosed with an autoimmune disease affecting my peripheral nervous system. In 1997 I found out I had prostate cancer. In 2005 I was diagnosed with a cancerous blood disorder. These days I totter about, can't type worth a damn, and have trouble with buttons. Otherwise much remains the same. I represent homeless people and victims of police misconduct. I continue to paint and draw and sculpt and write and protest.

＊ ＊ ＊

I am a Motherfucker no more. As I write, pale early morning sunlight illuminates what my letterhead dubs "the Law Offices of Osha Neumann," a small cluttered room in a fading orange Victorian on the corner of Martin Luther King Jr. Way in Berkeley, California. I've lived in Berkeley and North Oakland for over thirty years. I've raised my two daughters here. I have two granddaughters.

I am the sole employee, chief cook, and bottle washer of the Law Offices of Osha Neumann. My desk is forever covered with files of cases that won't go away and never seem to make any money. Law books lie open on the floor. On the wall over my computer are two of my paintings in black and white acrylic on paper: one depicts three hands shackled together, the other a policeman with a baton at a Black man's throat. On the wall opposite is a photograph of Diego Rivera working on a mural with brush in one hand, an enamel plate he's using as a pallet in the other. Above his photo on the wall are more of my paintings and a page from a weekly newspaper with my photograph in front of a shelf of law books. The newspaper named me a "local hero" and the blurb beneath the photo extols my various nefarious activities as muralist and legal defender of the poor. I am quoted as saying: "There is no good way to live these days, but the best way is in opposition."

Much has changed and much remains the same since my Motherfucker days on the Lower East Side. I still love a motherfuckeresque politics of disruption and confrontation. I look forward to the moment when the clash between us and them is in the open, when we cross the line into civil disobedience. I still define the essential struggle we are engaged in as a struggle against fascism, but I know that, despite what I assumed as a child, Jews are not always antifascist nor committed to the universality of truth. Sabra and Chatilla awakened me from my dogmatic slumber on the subject of the relation of Jews to fascism.

I am no longer plagued by my adolescent fantasies, but still suffer periodically from a crippling obsessiveness. I remain intrigued and puzzled by the relation of the personal to the political, and the mix of reason and irrationality in our politics. The issue of reason, its place in our political and personal lives, its limitations and its strengths, its purity and its perversions, still intrigues me.

* * *

In old movies, pages of a calendar on the wall flutter to the ground to indicate the passage of time. Off-camera, the actor is aged by the make-up artist. He re-appears with gray and thinning hair, wrinkles, liver spots and a bit of a pot.

Many pages have fluttered to the ground since the Sixties. Somehow, while those calendar pages were falling and my hair was turning white, and before I acquired an autoimmune disease and prostate cancer, a sea change occurred in my relationship with women, which corresponded to an equally profound change in my fantasy life. I was no longer plagued by fantasies of pain, of beating and being beaten. Those fantasies left like the symptoms of an illness that vanish when the fever breaks. They had flourished in the isolation of my body, in the absence of touch. And when I left the Motherfuckers to live with Yeshi, and when Rachel was born in a gush of blood, and we went to Black Bear, and fucked a lot, and worked naked in the hot sun, and when Emma was born eight years after Rachel I was touched, in body and spirit. In that touching, "the real" I had raged and clawed towards was given to me, gently, with tenderness and I was weaned, without even knowing it, from my sadomasochistic fantasies.

And no, I am not completely cured. I have retained from my childhood a sense of shame about the body, which takes the form of obsessions that well up suddenly and without warning, interrupting my colloquial relations with the world like an unwelcome creditor come to collect on a past due debt. Just as alcoholics in recovery never say that they are free of the disease, but begin every meeting by identifying themselves as alcoholics, so I must identify as a recovering . . . what? Self-flagellator? Misogynist? Perhaps a dual diagnosis is in order.

To a large extent the story of the Motherfuckers is the traditional story of men playing their dangerous, oh so important games, oblivious to women. Yeshi had been involved in civil rights and organizing years before I became actively political, and continued her organizing while I was Motherfuckering. She enters the story only as an appendage. After Rachel's birth at home she was inspired to become a midwife, and since then has assisted thousands of women to give birth. In her story the vagina is a not the focus of a hostile or lecherous gaze, but an opening to life and an inspiration for a vagina monologue—no, a vagina aria, a vagina chorus of massed voices singing hallelujah.

Motherfucker flier. "Henry" was our code name for a demonstration.

TODD GITLIN AND I—A SIXTIES FLASHBACK

From 1963 to 1965, Todd Gitlin was president of Students for a Democratic Society. In 1987 he published an ambitious history of the Sixties, *The Sixties, Years of Hope, Days of Rage*. His effort at capturing that decade is comprehensive, moderate in tone without being pedantic, and well written throughout. The book concludes with an eloquent attempt to honor what we achieved during that period of upheaval, while acknowledging our limitations. I particularly like the next to last sentence:

> On the one side, there remains the perennial trap of thinking old dilemmas can be outmuscled by the luck of youth; on the other, the trap of thinking the future is doomed to be nothing more than the past; between them possibly, the space to invent.

In 1985 Todd was teaching at the University of California in Berkeley. That year the campus was in turmoil, rocked by the largest and most militant demonstrations it had seen since the end of the Vietnam War. The goal of the demonstrations was to force the University to divest its holdings in companies that did business in South Africa. Demonstrators renamed Sproul Plaza, in the center of the campus, Biko Plaza, in honor of Stephen Biko, the martyred South African leader of the Black Consciousness movement. There were constant sit-ins in front of the system-wide administration building on Oxford Avenue. A group of primarily white activists broke away from the crowd at the end of a rally sponsored by the United People of Color and established an encampment on the steps of Sproul Hall, the campus administration building.

The wave of demonstrations was organized by a number of quite distinct groups. The divestment movement divided along fault lines of race and class. The encampment on the steps of Sproul Hall was primarily white. Student and non-student activists from the community mingled together, their numbers augmented by a shifting group of homeless street people. The organization of the encampment, if indeed it could be said to be organized at all, was tenuous at its best. Decision-making was an interminable process of reaching "consensus." The dysfunction of the street invaded the meetings. Some homeless person would invariably fall asleep, in the center of the circle, only to wake up agitated, ready to make a speech. African-American students who had organized separately were suspicious of the sometimes violently confrontational tone of the steps, and upset with the refusal by leaders of the vigil to acknowledge that African-American students had a right to lead a struggle that involved African liberation. Professors marched with dignity in support of the students, passed resolutions, and expressed solidarity.

I gravitated to the scene on the steps. I found the openness and craziness refreshing. I liked the disrespect, the push for confrontation, the breaking of rules. I liked the inclusion of the homeless, the drunk, and disorderly. I was also aware of the limitations.

As the year progressed there were hundreds of arrests as students and their supporters staged sit-ins blocking access to buildings. Ministers prayed as they were carted away. At one point the entire School Board of the City of Berkeley was arrested for blocking the entrance to the University-wide administration building. The rallies grew larger and larger. In the early morning hours of April 16, the police surrounded the encampment on the Sproul Hall steps and carted all 141 of us off to jail. The next day an enormous rally protesting the arrests filled Biko Plaza. Willie Brown, then speaker of the California State assembly, spoke in support of the demonstrators.

The movement was progressing in a classic pattern—the issue of divestment had broad appeal. Therefore those committed to the most aggressively confrontational tactics could push the entire process without alienating the more moderate sectors. Unfortunately, campus agitation is limited by the boundaries of the school year, and the end of the year was approaching. But an opportunity arose for one last hurrah before vacation. The Regents of the University of California had scheduled their June meeting to take place at the Lawrence Hall of Science, which is located in the Berkeley hills overlooking the campus. The subject of divestment was on their agenda.

The Lawrence Hall of Science is a squat domed structure of cement slabs that looks like a World War I bunker half buried in the hill. From the broad plaza that surrounds it, one is afforded a magnificent view of San Francisco bay. As the Regents met in the lecture hall in the basement, demonstrations swirled outside. The police were predictably brutal and out of hand—as they had been consistently throughout the year. There was a lot of shoving and pushing on both sides, but if you got tired of the battle you could present yourself at the police lines, and the police would let you through to go inside to observe the meeting. Which I did towards the beginning of the afternoon.

The audience was confined to a balcony overlooking the

stage of the auditorium on which the Regents were seated behind a long rectangular table. Before I arrived there had been substantive presentations on the situation in South Africa and the need for divestment, including an appeal from Pedro Noguera, student body president, and one of the leaders of the divestment movement. But by the time I took my seat the Regents were droning on and on, slouching toward the close of a meeting at which, predictably, they would do nothing.* A few of us, our adrenaline still pumping, began some mild heckling. As the meeting dribbled towards its inevitable conclusion, some of us stood up and yelled. We weren't loud enough or persistent enough to prevent the deliberations, but we did succeed, I thought, in introducing a little sense of risk and insecurity among the potentates. I was standing up in mid-heckle when, to my surprise, I felt a hand on my shoulder exerting a firm downward pressure to force me back into my seat. At the same time I heard the person behind me say in the voice of a vexed junior high school teacher: "Oh Tom [surely he knew I had changed my name to Osha years ago], cut it out." or something to that effect. I turned around and there was Todd Gitlin, frowning at me disapprovingly. I instantly reverted to my Motherfucker persona and hissed back at him: "Get your fucking hands off me," or something, I hoped, equally menacing. He didn't touch me again. I yelled a few more times, just to show I wasn't intimidated. The meeting ended. We filed out. Todd and I studiously avoiding looking at each other.

Which brings me back to Todd's penultimate sentence. "On the one side, there remains the perennial trap of thinking old dilemmas can be outmuscled by the luck of youth; on the other, the trap of thinking the future is doomed to be nothing

* A year later, they adopted a policy of phased full divestment from companies doing business in South Africa.

more than the past; between them possibly, the space to invent."

That sentence has such a fine balance: "On the one side," and "on the other," and then the suggestion of a synthesis "between them *possibly* [emphasis added] the space to invent." I can imagine Todd got up from his desk after writing that sentence feeling very satisfied with himself, as well he should have. The tone is tentative, wise, careful. The voice is that of one no longer prey to enthusiasms, but still committed.

Many of us would like to think of ourselves that way. But the truth is more complicated. We are uneasy. We feel that despite our best efforts we have been trapped, accepting the unacceptable, compromising with the intolerable. I suspect that Todd saw in the gray-haired figure that rose in front of him at the Regents meeting, blocking his view of the proceedings, the embodiment of the mindless juvenile narcissistic anarchism, narrow and irrational, which he blamed in part for the Left's inability to create a broad movement of opposition. And I, turning back towards him, saw the comfortably positioned professor. While I felt some pleasure in the thought that I had retained (better than he) the basic instinct of disrespect, I wondered if I lacked his ability to grow up, and whether I would remain constantly trapped in infantile exhibitions of anger at authority.

In truth, I could never write a book like Todd's. There are some activities which I have found almost impossible to perform without appearing ridiculous: rushing around airports with heavy luggage is one; finding a place to pee in a strange city is another. And writing about the Sixties is yet another. The project requires me to look at the trajectory of life that had a period of revolutionary exaltation (or so I remember it) at the beginning, and something far more ambiguous, and in some ways less satisfactory, in the present. The person whom I was then looks back at me now and defies me to justify my current compromised life, and the person I am now looks back on the infantile grandiosity of the period and is embarrassed. Stalemate.

The Sixties were marked by an unrelenting urgency. The very act of reflecting sometimes feels like a betrayal. To reflect is to step back. To step back is to disengage. By ceasing to battle even for a moment, the project to which we were committed is defeated. It lies by the side of the historical road, picked over by scavengers, eaten by scholastic ants, parceled out and dissected, an occasion for sentimental soliloquies, the inspiration for collections of memorabilia, a commodity.

Back then we were intolerant of bystanders. We had a slogan: "If you're not part of the solution, your part of the problem." The slogan was coined by Eldridge Cleaver, a convicted rapist and Minister of Information for the Black Panther Party, who died after becoming at various times a dope addict, a Mooney, and a small time hustler for various right-wing causes. I remember seeing him on the weekends selling odd junk at the Berkeley Flea Market. An American flag and a California flag flanked his stall. Whether he thought of himself as part of the problem or part of the solution no one cared to ask.

The historian comfortably ensconced in academia was not, I used to think, part of the solution. Now, somewhat mellowed—despite my interaction with Todd—I am more accepting, and wouldn't mind a comfortable academic job myself. I'm a little jealous of him. Many of my friends have become, like me, hyphenated radicals: radical-doctors, radical-lawyers, radical-therapists. The hyphen does not result in excommunication from the congregation of solutions. There are not always such clear distinctions between problems and solutions. They intertwine like lovers.

MY SIXTIES PROBLEM

My Sixties problem is simply stated. I was a Motherfucker. I have to come to grips with all the strengths and terrible weaknesses of the Motherfuckers. I can't glorify or discount what we did back then. I have to write without nostalgia or disdain.

The hippie counter-culture of the Sixties has melted away. What's left is a residue of trivial curiosities: tie-dyed shirts, psychedelic posters, aging rock stars—hardly an impressive legacy. The flower children we sought to politicize bloomed for a brief season then faded and dropped their petals. They were not perennials. The Motherfucker strain of the counter-culture did not outlive them, though perhaps remnants of it, largely depoliticized, survived in punk. We quickly self-destructed, a victim of our own rhetoric. We were hurtling towards death with such obvious relish that all but the most suicidal potential converts kept their distance.

I did not become a Motherfucker because I lacked privilege. I had more than enough privilege. Nor had I experienced material deprivation. Never in my life had I gone hungry. I experienced my oppression as an inability to touch reality. Endless introspection only separated me further from the world. I felt everything outside myself to be without substance, denatured, unreal. Nothing held together: Thought existed in isolation from experience, intellect from emotion, reason from reality. Living with these separations contributed to a diminished sense of the reality of my own being, which in turn sucked the substance from things, desiccating the apple on the bough, bleaching the sunset, turning rivers into trickles of dust. The face life turned to me was a lie. I was lost in a labyrinth of thin disguises.

. In revolt against the experience of unreality, I joined the swelling tide of rebels and drop outs. We would bring the war home. We were determined to provoke the system to shed all its disguises and expose its true nature. It would reveal itself as the policeman's club, the steel bars of a cell, perhaps ultimately a bullet heading our way. I wrote in my journal:

> We live in an unreproducable zero, surrounded by husks of representation. The unreality is held together by its images. The less substantial it becomes in itself, the more images are required to hold it together.
>
> The essence of America is that it is zero. It has already been wiped out. The war is over. By going into the streets and fighting cops we create our enemy. We make something to fight against. We call it into existence. As long as America doesn't exist it is invincible. We will have won when we have fully created our enemy, when we have forced him into a body. And we seem to be able to do this only by totally encircling him with violence. And the same with us. Violence gives us for the first time a body. And that body fills in the present by being beaten. Experience must be attached to a body that is being beaten or feels itself as potentially beaten.

As a child I had fantasized a strong father who would beat me if I was bad. I imagined his whippings as pleasure compared with the psychological torture of my relation to my mother. As a Motherfucker, I imagined violence as redemptive and necessary for personal and political transformation.

* * *

The Russian, Chinese, and Cuban revolutions, along with the struggles against colonial domination in Africa and Latin America, shaped our imagery of revolution. They were revolutions of the exploited and disenfranchised. They were nationalist movements against foreign domination. Often led by the educated children of the middle class, they mobilized peasants and workers whose revolt was fueled by material scarcity. But in the Sixties, the privileged children of white America revolted as much against "having" as against "not having." The scarcity we revolted against was not a material scarcity. Our hunger for nourishment differed from the hunger of Ethiopians, but was hunger nevertheless. It was an emptiness in the midst of material abundance, a starvation of the spirit.

I imagined that people who are materially oppressed did not experience identity crises. For Blacks in the diamond mines of South Africa, Vietnamese in their rice paddies, Cubans in their sugar cane fields, identity was not a problem because the source of their oppression was clearly external. They did not experience themselves as struggling towards "the real." The reality of the world was inescapable. But for me, revolt was a continual process of trying to rid myself of an inner emptiness, to cough it up, to get it out of my system, to become "real" so that I could "be in touch with reality." If I succeeded in becoming part of the revolution it would become clear who and what I was. I would become whole. Revolution as therapy.

The politicized counterculture that developed in the youth ghettoes of the Sixties was built on a set of correlations. That portion of our selves which society sought to *repress*, we identified with those whom society *oppressed*. The violence of our rages against our parents we identified with the violent rage of the colonized against the colonizer. But despite our assertions of solidarity with the oppressed around the world, the qualitative differences in our struggles remained. We gagged on our piece of pie while others still struggled to get to the table. We dropped out; others were never offered the opportunity to drop in. Our commitment to revolution seemed a matter of choice; theirs, a necessity.

No one would say of the Blacks or the Vietnamese, or the bearded Cubans in the Sierra Meistra that their struggle was "only a stage." But that charge was continually leveled against us. We were immature. Our colorful motley was the peach fuzz of adolescence, which we would sooner or later exchange for the drab conformist plumage of the adult of the species. We vehemently denied that our revolt was any bit less authentic than that of the colonized peoples with whom we declared our solidarity, but how could we refute that accusation? Only time would tell to what extent age would dim our enthusiasm for revolution. And I'm not sure time has come to our defense.

The poor and the dispossessed struggle against hunger and disease. They are famished. It is not for them to elaborate a critique of the cuisine that is not on their plates. That critique, the critique of the misuse of abundance, was our job. Or so we thought. But the commodity culture we detested has spread across the globe. It penetrates everywhere and everywhere generates resistance. Mud huts are turned into internet cafés. Satellite dishes sprout from corrugated tin roofs in the favelas, ghettoes and refugee camps of Asia and Africa and Latin America. Inside, in the gloom, the TV glows and the poor peer, as through a window, at an ever-changing tableau of the richest, and purportedly most sexually attractive, athletic, talented and famous people in the world. On display are all the accoutrements of a life worth living—designer jeans with prestigious labels on the butt, sneakers endorsed by the best athletes, cars that purr like kittens, beers that melt away inhibitions, deodorants that mask life's unpleasant odors, entertaining breakfast cereals, rejuvenating soft drinks.

In the Third World, those who are exploited as producers are courted as consumers. Luxurious commodities are advertised on crumbling walls where donkeys drowse and pigs root for rubbish. The West sucks product from the Third World and sends back addicting images of an unobtainable lifestyle. One form that resistance takes to this flood of colonizing images is fundamentalism. Fundamentalism is born of disgust with what passes in the West as progressive, modern, and rational.* We, the privileged drop-outs in the West, had our own critique of what passes for reason and progress. But while fundamentalists in the Third World extol a return to traditional values, we had nothing to which we wanted to return. We were inventing a new way of being, incommensurate in every way with the lives our parents led. Our revolution would be a spontaneous outburst without precedent, expressed in a language that mobilized the imagination towards the goal of an utter and complete renewal of the world.

We tried to build an ersatz counter-culture on the spot—with mixed results. Though we rejected the authority of the

---

* As the Northern Alliance entered Herat, a city in Northern Afghanistan, the Taliban fled leaving behind in the Ministry for the Promotion of Virtue and Prevention of Vice a hardcover copy of a Taliban Penal Code, containing a list of "unclean things." These included: "pork, pig, pig oil, anything made from human hair, satellite dishes, cinematography, any equipment that produces the joy of music, pool tables, chess, masks, alcohol, tapes, computers, VCR's, televisions, anything that propagates sex and is full of music, wine, lobster, nail polish, firecrackers, statues, sewing catalogues, pictures, Christmas cards" (Amy Waldman, *New York Times*, "Taliban penal code defined virtue vice," November 22, 2001).

past, we searched the pre-industrial world for models on which to base our post-industrial lives. We were a tribe, a clan, a band of nomads. We were Indian mystics, Tantric monks, or Mexican brujos. We were moving resolutely back to the future.

With drugs we went spelunking into the branching caves of our unconsciousness and rocketing out into infinite space. We dissolved into a shower of atoms. We merged with fish and birds and clouds and folds of fabric. I first took acid at Bryn Athen, an organic farm in Vermont run by folks who were friends with some of the Motherfuckers. I sat down in the grass of a pasture with Yeshi. As the acid came on I saw the hills begin to move like the backs of dinosaurs. Later we fucked and my body exploded into incandescent particles of pleasure. Afterwards, as we lay together on an open sleeping platform, I worried that the people walking by in the distance were a disapproving posse of "Vermont Freudians." Not everyone's trip was so benign. During a riot on St. Marks Place, a kid running from the police in a demonstration told me he saw his body riddled with bullets and his blood running onto the pavement. And within a fortnight of Angry Arts week, a young boy newly arrived on the Lower East Side, went up onto the roof, saw wings sprouting from his shoulder blades, and jumped to his death on the sidewalk.

The Motherfuckers fought with the police and experimented with LSD, attempting by any means necessary to break through old habits of obedience and perception. Common sense was a facade. Nothing common made sense. I felt we were immersed in unreality like a fetus in its amniotic sack. We needed to break through that sack to be born again out of the "belly of the beast." We were the children of that beast turning on our mother—destroying her, ripping her apart in the process of our birth. We were fucking her from inside out. One current of the counter-culture was about blissed-out being. But the Motherfuckers seemed to be about penetration, the penetration of the prisoner through the wall of his cell, the penetration of the birthing infant through the vagina, the penetration of the rapist, angry and violent. Revolution as sex crime.

* * *

Revolution as sex crime? What madness.

Three times, while the first and second Intifadas were raging, I traveled to Palestine. Each time Palestinian doctors led us through hospital wards, where silent mothers sat by the bedside of their children. We would stop first at one bed, then another. The doctors would hold back the sheets so we could see the wounds. They would ask those children who were awake and not in too much pain to explain what had happened to them. I remember a twelve-year-old boy telling us how the Israeli soldiers methodically broke all his limbs, first his arms, then his legs.

On my first trip to Gaza, our delegation met with doctors who drove us to the Jabaliya refugee camp. They guided us through narrow alleys, twisting between bare concrete walls that led to a succession of small courtyards. From the courtyards, doorways opened onto a succession of rooms. The rooms were dark and smelled of blood. In each of the rooms that we visited we met people who showed us their wounds. In one room we met six Palestinian women lying on mats. They had all been beaten. Defying taboos they began to undo their black embroidered dresses. They showed us their arms, blue with bruises. In another room a woman showed us a dark bloodstain on the wall where Israeli soldiers had shot her husband as he sat next to her on the couch.

How could I tell the children in the hospital, the women in Gaza, or the exhausted Palestinian doctors who so patiently answered all our questions that I had been a Motherfucker? Or that violence was a means of getting in touch with reality?

In the Third World, and in the ghettos of the First, the colonial power that attacks the family also attacks the body politic. It sets itself up as the illegitimate head of household. It is the enemy of the motherland and of the mother. The revolutionary in the Third World fights for the right to grow up, to come to full manhood or womanhood, to be respected, to parent the next generation, to inherit the home.

In Central and South America, revolutionaries love their mothers. I traveled to Nicaragua while the Sandinistas were in power. I saw posters showing a revolutionary fighter embracing his mother and urging respect for the mothers of the revolution. The Mothers of the Disappeared and the Mothers of Revolutionary Martyrs are given the highest place in the revolutionary pantheon. I imagine that guerrillas hiding in safe houses, or clinging to the sides of volcanoes, long for their mothers and their deepest wish is to give them a better life, to protect them, and keep them from harm's way.

Central American revolutionaries defend the mother. They are strengthened by her love, and saved by it from guilt at defying the paternal authority of the dictator. I was angry at my mother. I could not invoke her love in my struggle with the system. In struggling against the system I renewed my struggle against her. I rebelled against her and longed for her maternal embrace.

* * *

I have heard it said that the phrase, "The personal is political," first gained currency in the women's movement of the early Seventies. But under a banner emblazoned with that slogan, we Motherfuckers whipped ourselves toward ever more encompassing commitment. We strove to break down the barriers between our personal and political life, with the paradoxical effect that the personal was made visible at the same time that it tended to disappear into the politics. I don't think I was the only one aware that the emotions we poured into our politics were derived, in part from our personal histories. We were driven as much by private need as by moral imperative. But we did not care to dwell on that distinction for fear of creating a separation that would leave our politics without the fuel of passion, and our personal lives without the possibility of redemption.

The Motherfuckers were not unique in striving to obliterate the line between the personal and the political. In many parts of the movement, activists exposed the most intimate details of their daily life to criticism and correction. Old living arrangements were obstacles to the revolution. We experimented with new ones. We formed communes and lived collectively. We conducted campaigns to smash monogamy, couplism, heterosexism, and the nuclear family. We permitted a totalitarian intrusion of the "movement" into personal life. We condemned privacy. Everything was open to public scrutiny and comment—from the way we brushed our teeth to the way we fucked.

But in all of this examination of personal life, secrets were kept. And in those secret places contradictions festered. Proclaiming that it was time to give ourselves unreservedly to the roaring flood of revolution, we hid the anchors that bound us to the past. Proclaiming that we were prepared to collectivize all our possessions, we who came from the middle class concealed from our working class brothers and sisters the trust funds and inheritances we knew would come our way. We fooled ourselves as much as we fooled the enemy. We planted private gardens. And when our secrets became too many and the hold of ideology waned, we quietly left the movement to resume work on deferred personal agendas.

* * *

In the Sixties we tended to call the institutionalized power we were fighting, together with the ideological and cultural baggage that went along with it, "The System."[26] We thought of it as a monolith. In the intervening years "The System" has become, if anything, more monolithic while our movements of opposition have disintegrated, and seem to have lost the thread of common purpose. I have learned to celebrate diversity— and am glad for it—but have more difficulty finding the basis for unity. The possibility of a shared truth has been called into question. Reason is too closely associated with dead white men to be considered a reliable guide in matters of the heart—or politics. I and many others have soldiered on, but for many years we have not been moist with hope. We inhabit a dry arroyo with the name of a terrible woman: "TINA—There Is No Alternative." We shout into the emptiness, "A Better World is Possible" and wait for an answering echo.

"What's left?" I've wondered. What's left of the left?" In my worst moments, it seems only shards and fragments.

For me and many of my comrades transitions have not been easy. When the Sixties ended somewhere in the early Seventies we entered a period of lost momentum. We left a period of revolutionary enthusiasm, no matter how misguided it may have been at times, and entered into an extended doldrums, a lull between the storms. Our vision clouded, our flock dispersed. I'm still called an activist, although I don't much like the term. What sort of "activity" do activists do? We do not call a violinist an "activist" though her fingers hold the bow and move "actively" up and down the neck of her instrument.

For the activist all causes are interchangeable. Racism, environmental destruction, imperialist wars, sexist advertising, each is proxy for all the others. "Flower in the crannied wall," mused Tennyson, "if I could understand / what you are, root and all, and all in all, / I should know what God and man is."[27] For the activist, each cause is a flower in a crannied wall that unfolds into a universe within which it is linked to all others.

There is always a tension between politics' collective thrust and the irreducible aloneness in which we inhabit our subjectivity. We all carry truths that do not fit in, that undermine our commitment, that contradict our professed beliefs. We carry them as symptom and obsession and secret anxiety. In times of uncertain direction and muted resistance, powerful currents of opposition are not available to pull us from our isolation.

Stranded on the shore by the receding tide of revolution, many of us survivors of the Sixties left "the movement"—or felt that the movement had left us—and returned to career paths we had abandoned in our inflamed enthusiasm for the struggle. What use was a career if we were destined to die on the barricades? Many of the children of the middle class went back to school, obtained degrees, and entered professions. Meanwhile *the* movement splintered into many movements: liberation movements of women, gays, lesbians, bisexuals, transgendered, and the disabled; movements to oppose the use of nuclear power and the development of nuclear weapons; movements to protect the environment; movements to support guerrilla struggles in Central and Latin America; and each time the United States went to war, a movement to stop that war. While the movement splintered, the system we opposed did not. The Soviet Union collapsed. For all its faults, it had represented an antipode to global capitalism. Control of all aspects of human life on this planet fell increasingly into the hands of one superpower and the multinational corporations whose interests it faithfully serves and defends. Not until the series of demonstrations against the institutions of consolidated global capitalism that began in November 1999 in Seattle, did I feel that there was again a movement that could become the shared expression of our collective dream of liberation. And then came 9/11. We'd rallied outsides the citadels of capitalism. Mohammad Atta and his crew, with their volatile mix of fundamentalism and jet fuel, blew them up. The twin towers crumbled into dust, and I knew our job had been made more difficult.

* * *

For the Motherfuckers and huge sections of the movement it was not enough to join hands, sway back and forth, and sing with half shut eyes: "We shall overcome *someday*." Our slogan was "Freedom Now!" Freedom could not to be deferred. "Now" meant right now. The experience of freedom needed to be part of the struggle for freedom. A movement for freedom which modeled what it meant to be free would grow by shining example.

The key tactic for incorporating the experience of freedom into the struggle for liberation was civil disobedience. When we disobeyed the authority of the state, there came briefly into existence a space we experienced as a zone of genuine freedom. In everyday life the forces of repression are omnipresent but generally invisible and unfelt. Violence is held in suspension like droplets of water in a cloud. Civil disobedience precipitated those forces out of suspension. They arrayed themselves against us, and in so doing assumed a definite shape and occupied a definable space. Once that space was defined, we could take our stand outside it. Where we took our stand—be it at the segregated lunch counter, the doorway of the army recruiting center, or the corner of St. Marks Place and 2nd Avenue—was liberated territory.

Many of us felt for the first time what it meant to be free, at precisely the moment that our freedom was taken way from us. In jail, locked behind bars, we felt vulnerable and at peace. Singing freedom songs as the handcuffs were placed on our wrist, we felt joy and fear together. Torn from family and friends, we felt community. We had chosen life and it surged through us in the face of death and danger. We felt real. The moment had an undeniable self-evident rightness. The experience was addictive.

The power of these experiences sustained the civil rights movement and inspired the antiwar movement. They were a gift we cherished. But they were a deceptively simple gift. A movement could not offer people such moments without a means for fulfilling their promise. Once the genie was out of the bag, we did not want to put her back. People could not be convinced to settle for less. The thirst for liberation gave energy but undermined form. Few structures and organizations have survived from the Sixties. We never developed a strategy, a political culture or an organization that could preserve the promise of those moments. Liberation requires, as Antonio Gramsci wrote in his *Prison Diaries,* a "long march through the institutions." The movement will have to defer some promises while retaining its intransigent core. Such a movement can not be built overnight. We have yet to create a movement that can preserve the molten promise of freedom while tempering it so that it becomes hard and durable. We do not yet have a movement that can bridge the gap, a gap perhaps of generations, between the foretaste of freedom and its realization. We can not simultaneously shout "freedom now" and "freedom not quite yet."

* * *

The white counter-culture of the Sixties, with the anti-war movement at its political core, drew converts by the promise that within it one could experience what it meant to be free. The movement was a liberated zone. Liberation meant liberation from the stultifying restrictions of bourgeois life, from parents and surrogate parents. It meant sexual freedom. It meant we could slough off our old identities as a snake sloughs its skin. We could grow our hair long; throw away our button down collars and pantyhose; dress, not for success, but for revolution; and choose a new name, a nom de guerre. Our images of personal transformation came from a variety of sources. The Southern Civil Rights movement was one. The guerrilla movements of Latin America were another. Che and Fidel left the comforts of home and took to the mountains. When they came down out of the mountains, bearded, cigar smoking, dressed in green fatigues, they looked different and they had been changed—changed utterly. A "new man" had been forged and tempered in battle.

In strange amalgam, the image of the revolutionary transformed by the revolution fused with acid fueled visions in which all things melted and morphed, all permanence dissolved, and nothing withstood change. "Better living through chemistry" proclaimed a tongue in cheek poster of the time. LSD would dissolve the old self and allow a radical new being to emerge. With typical American hubris we believed we could be anybody: Zen monk, Mexican *brujo*, Sioux medicine man.

We imagined ourselves the heroes in a revolutionary version of a Horatio Alger story. Horatio's heroes pulled themselves up from rags to riches by tugging on their bootstraps. We thought we could transform ourselves by pulling in the opposite direction—down from the heights of privilege, away from its constraints, and into the future. All that was required was the willingness to set off on the adventure.

* * *

The movement's emphasis on the transformation of personal life was charismatic, but, at the same time, it limited participation. Not everyone was ready for an intrusive political movement that accepted only total commitment. Not everyone was prepared to have his or her bedroom and bathroom transformed into a terrain of political struggle. The more global and universal the definition of the revolutionary project, the fewer, ultimately, were those who could—or would—meet its stringent demands. The perfect recruit for the revolution was a young rootless dropout, with lots of time on his or her hands and no commitments. The movement became the whole of life for those who joined it. It was a life cut off from the daily life of ordinary working people, with jobs, families, and children.

As we expanded the definition of what was political we simultaneously narrowed the area of what we considered legitimate political action. All those activities that were not total, that did not call into question the very existence of those who participated, were illegitimate. Any act that lacked the element of ultimate risk was hopelessly compromised. Electoral politics, letter writing, peaceful demonstrations confined within the barricades set up by the police, were worse than useless. Civil disobedience became progressively less civil.

Only a total transformation of society would do. And the only organization worthy of allegiance was one that was committed to that total transformation and which required from its members a corresponding total commitment. These organizations risked becoming cults, tense pressure cookers in which their members were largely isolated from the everyday life of ordinary people.

* * *

Infantile rage is a fuel that is easily exhausted. It will not sustain a lifetime of commitment. Only structure in the personality and organization in the movement allows growth over time. We need organizations that are capable of exercising some authority but avoid reproducing the authoritarian modes of the dominant society. We need organizations that can link generations, providing a way for revolutionary Peter Pans to grow up. Without such institutions, "growing up" will continue to seem an inevitable conspiracy of biology with the forces of reaction.

The movement of the Sixties sought to reveal denied truths, not by developing a comprehensive theory, but in molten hand to hand struggle with the system of lies in which we lived. By joining that struggle, we believed we were placing ourselves where truth lived. We broadened the zone of political activity in all directions—inward into the "personal" and outward into a critique of daily life. The System was an integrated totality that subordinated all aspects of experience to its destructive purposes. The transformation of that system would transform the deep structures of society—and of consciousness. The false smile of commodities would be extinguished. The real face of the world would emerge, washed in possibilities.

By defying the System we would force the truth into the open. All would be revealed in an ecstasy of clarity. The System was a lie. We stood for truth. It was ugly. We were beautiful. It was evil. We stood for justice. It was a prison. We would be free. It was irrational. We were supremely sane.

But, of course, there were murky edges to our ecstasy of clarity. Our vision attracted craziness as shiny bobbles attract magpies, as the open flame attracts moths. Having seen so many revolutionary moths crashing into the flame, many of us have reexamined our rhetoric and tempered our expectations. We purged as an infantile aberration the extravagant imagination of unlimited possibilities that inspired our most heroic—or foolhardy—acts of disobedience. But the vision doesn't really die. The wet dream of possibilities imagined by the counterculture of the Sixties is real, even now, as we struggle to avert an equally real nightmare: fascist regression, the triumph of unreason, the death of nature, the extinction of hope. Our flame smolders underground, waiting for the wind that will fan it back to fury.

Nothing to lose but our chains.

THE PURSUIT OF TRUTH AS AN UNVEILING

Workers of the world unite! You have nothing to lose but your chains.

—Karl Marx, *The Communist Manifesto*

I once was lost but now am found
Was blind, but now I see.

—John Newton, "Amazing Grace"

Imagine the condition of men living in a sort of cavernous chamber underground, with an entrance open to the light and a long passage all down the cave. Here they have been from childhood, chained by the leg and also by the neck, so that they can not turn their heads.

—Plato, *The Republic*, Chapter XXV (VII. 514 A-521 B),
The Allegory of the Cave

The Motherfuckers on St. Marks Place, philosophers in their dens, therapists in their offices, penitents in their confessionals, artists in their studios, all strive to reveal a hidden truth, be it the brutality of the System, the unexamined assumption, the repressed desire, the sinful act, the form within the flux. They all, in one way or another, seek to strip away the disguises worn by reality. In order to truly see, we must be free from the whip of the overseer, from illusion, from neurotic symptom, from sin, from conventional forms of perception. The connection between the throwing off of chains and the unveiling of truth is implicit in Plato's allegory, Marx's battle cry, and the hymn of the sea captain who is done with the slave trade and longing for grace.

Insofar as truth is hidden, we are unfree. Insofar as we are unfree, we are kept from the truth. And insofar as the rebel, the philosopher, the therapist, the priest, and the artist promise to liberate us, once and for all, they fail. The world the rebel hopes to free remains enslaved, the truth the philosopher hopes to reveal slips from his grasp, the patient on the therapist's couch remains unhappy, the penitent sins again, the beauty the artist creates remains locked within the frame. Our efforts to reveal and uncover become themselves disguises and concealment. Our struggle never ends.

* * *

Schoolchildren will rip out their desks and throw ink at stunned instructors, office secretaries will disrobe and run into the streets, newsboys will rip up their newspapers and sit on the curbstones masturbating, storekeepers will throw open their doors making everything free, accountants will all collapse in one mighty heart attack, soldiers will throw down their guns.

—Abbie Hoffman[28]

The movements of the Sixties, at least those in which I participated, strove to undermine the foundations of the System and thereby liberate repressed truths and possibilities. Disruption, transgression, and violation of boundaries, were preconditions for a fresh encounter with reality. Explosive energy was needed to break the public and private fetters that prevented us from reaching the truth. In struggle with the System we would strip away disguises, unveil the naked truth, and show that the emperor had no clothes. When we ceased to be obedient, the masks would drop, not only from the faces of our treacherous leaders, but from the ordinary and familiar face that the world turned to us in our day-to-day. Our true friends, our real enemies, hidden horror and concealed beauty would be revealed.

As a child I listened to the dinner table conversations of my parents and came to believe that reason was the ultimate test of truth and the sole instrument of its discovery. In the Sixties I came to a different conclusion: Truth was hidden. It would be revealed through action. I was impatient with theory. It was more important to be raging in the streets than studying in the library.

I was not alone in my impatience. Students in the university were abandoning their classes impatient with theory that had no visible relation to practice. Reason was a shrinking violet, fearful of violence and loud noises. Reason did not provide a reliable map of the terrain of revolution. It was useless in probing the weak spots of the enemy. Analysis, study, large theories, and explanations involving a great deal of reading, ultimately resulted in inaction, or the irrelevant gesturing of the Old Left. In other parts of the movement they may have read books on the theory of revolution and the nature of capitalism. In my corner we read next to nothing.

* * *

When I dropped out of graduate school to become a painter and went to live on the Lower East Side of Manhattan, I felt myself letting go of the thread of reason that kept me from sinking into the underworld of those who *experience*, but do not *know*. Angry with my mother, filled with self-loathing, I exiled myself from my parents' world.

In exile, the image of the homeland remains fixed and immutable. The blasphemer, by the vehemence of his blasphemies, reveals the continuing power of his faith. In my exile

I have been the model of piety. I may have rebelled against reason, but my apostasy, even then, was never complete. Amidst all the fervent unreasonableness of the Sixties, I would have fallen into despair, had I allowed myself to believe that what I was doing was not in the service of reason. I wore the disguise of a crazy Motherfucker, but I thought our goal was completely rational: to oppose with the utmost energy an insane destructive menace and to awaken concealed and denied possibilities for happiness.

We might have appeared unreasonable, but we were not irrational. Finally, and with great difficulty, I have come to realize that the images of Auschwitz and of my father's book-lined study do not suffice to express the polarity of reason and the irrational.

There is a difference between irrationality and non-rationality. Reason falls silent before the melody sung by an open window, the jamboree of color in a mountain meadow, the lovers shedding their clothes as they make their way to bed. There is nothing irrational about art, music, or the beauty of nature. Quite the contrary. Irrationality is a wild upsurge of destructive temper, in nations and in people. To foul one's own nest, to hurt oneself or those one loves is irrational. As opposed to the irrational, the non-rational is rationality's silent mirror, a model for the right ordering of the world.[29]

THE PROMISE OF HAPPINESS

One evening, a number of years back, I was sitting at my desk in my office when I heard music coming from the street outside my window. I got up and went out onto the front porch. A few yards down the block four men were standing in a loose circle on the sidewalk under a street lamp. They were singing a gospel song in four-part harmony. I have sometimes seen egrets standing in the slough by the side of the freeway, all elegance and grace, in the muck and stagnant water. Their song was like a gorgeous migratory bird that had chosen our block to rest awhile. The men's voices were the best of friends. They could not have been better suited to each other had they dreamt each other into being. "I was lost, my sweet brother," each voice said, "and you have found me." A car stopped. A woman asked what church they belonged to, and complemented them. She sat for a while, listening with the window rolled down, resting her head on the steering wheel. And I stood on the porch, suddenly and unexpectedly happy.

Their song made everything all right. It opened a space within which a fragrant grove sprung up, and we were brought in among its sheltering boughs. The men sang for a while, and then they stopped and continued on their way and when their song ended the space the song created closed up again. And we were left to our own devices.

Most of the time we take our relationship to things—lampposts, sidewalks, doorways, telephones, keyboards, billboards, baskets of laundry—for granted. We expect little of them, and they give back little in return. They tend to be just there, giving us at best a flaccid handshake, staring at us blankly as if they didn't know us. Numerous, monotonous, lacking in conviction, things press up close against each other but avoid touching, like strangers in a crowded elevator. Art allows us to touch the inner thigh of things. It turns a marriage of convenience between the self and the world into an extravagant love

The Promise of Happiness.

affair. The partner we have long since ceased to admire and cherish becomes the embodiment of our dreams.

"Art," wrote Stendhal, "is the promise of happiness."[30] Politics, like art, should be a promise of happiness, the promise that the space a song can open up will not disappear when the song stops. At times, running in the streets during a demonstration, I have felt something of that promise, the same promise I felt in that song those men sang as I listened on the porch of my office.

* * *

Seattle. November, 1999. Demonstration against the World Trade Organization. I am running or rather hobbling through clouds of tear gas and pepper spray, feeling my old Motherfucker love of riots rekindled. My eyes burn. Tears stream down my face, obscuring my vision. Behind us the police are hurling concussion grenades and shooting rubber bullets into the crowd. I pass a young man. He's just standing there. He's been wounded just below his lower lip by a rubber bullet. It has made a hole through to his gums. I look back to see a line of police advancing. They are dressed in black and encased entirely in bulky body armor. Their movements are jerky and stiff like the monsters in old Frankenstein movies. Their faces are hidden by the visors of their helmets. Behind them comes an armored riot control vehicle. A cop is standing on its hood, firing what looks like a mutant Gatling gun with a cluster of revolving barrels.

In the lulls between attacks by the police I have time to wander through downtown Seattle. The stores are deserted. Our hand-painted banners hang from their balconies. Many of their windows were broken early in the morning by a roving band of anarchists—the dreaded "Black Block"—shouting slogans and concealing their faces with bandannas. I recognize them. They're the modern day Motherfuckers, reveling in the sound of breaking glass.[31] I admire the shattered windows of the Starbucks outlet, Niketown, and the Gap.

On the corner of the FAO Schwartz megastore, adjacent to an enormous two story high bronze teddy bear, someone has spray painted "We are winning." We *are* winning. Or so it seems. We have prevented one of the most powerful organizations on earth from holding its meeting. We have held Madeleine Albright, the secretary of state of the world's dominant superpower, a virtual prisoner in her hotel room. And we have all, it seemed to me, been aroused to a great aliveness by the threat of danger and the thrill of victory.

Late in the afternoon, I stop at an intersection to watch a group of young, mostly brown-skinned women (the demonstrators have been predominantly white) dancing in the middle of an intersection. As they dance, they sing:

> Wood, Stone, Feather and Bone,
> Roar of the ocean guide us home.
> River, Sea, Ancient Tree,
> Howl of the wind gonna set us free.

On "Roar" they extend their arms in front of them. On "Howl," they reach towards the sky and spread their hands. On each word they move in unison and turn—back, forward, left, right—accompanied by a young man drumming on a dumbec. They laugh as they move and smile at us and take time to teach us the words. They are vigorous, graceful, open, and nonviolent—everything the Robocops are not. I find them achingly beautiful. The moment is fragile. I know it can't last. Soon the intersection will be overrun by police. But for now the dancing has made it ours. And I think and feel—there is no higher art, no greater reason, no better politics, no other place on earth I'd rather be.

A HIDEOUS RATIONALITY

"[The] idea of Reason comprehends everything and ultimately absolves everything, because it has its place and function in the whole and the whole is beyond good and evil, truth and falsehood. It may even be justifiable, logically as well as historically, to define Reason in terms which include slavery, the Inquisition, child labor, concentration camps, gas chambers, and nuclear preparedness. These may well have been integral parts of that rationality which has governed the recorded history of mankind.

—Herbert Marcuse, "A Note on Dialectic"
preface to *Reason and Revolution*[32]

"Be reasonable," we are told if our demands upon the System become too insistent, our voices too strident. By which is meant: Be patient. Defer gratification. Acquiesce. Play by the rules. Do not rock the boat. In short—accept the limits of the possible as defined by the System. The patronizing voice of reason whispers in our ear to mind our manners. But in a world hurtling towards nightmare, it is not irrational to be unreasonable.

The increasing rationality of the System is accompanied by an increasing irrationality. The more complete the System's ability to control our lives, the more it spirals out of control. Science furnishes the tools by which people and things are manipulated, without commenting on how those tools are used. It prepares the world for exploitation as a nurse prepares a patient for her examination. The nurse takes her clothing from the patient leaving her near naked and shivering in one of those flimsy paper gowns that tie awkwardly in the back. Science takes from nature the clothing of subjectivity, leaving her bare and unprotected. It reduces quality to quantity just as business translates all value into dollars.[33]

The claim of reason to universality becomes a disguise for the System's self-serving agenda. The naked pursuit of profit is unseemly. As conquistadors slaughtered under the banner of the universal religion of Christ, so modern nations slaughter under the banner of universal reason. Reason may not be directly invoked, but the children she bore in the eighteenth century—the liberal ideals of representative government and individual freedom—are constantly trotted out as justifications for the theft of resources, the destruction of trade barriers, and the imposition of market discipline. "This is our opportunity to provide an impetus to freedom and democracy in Latin America and create new jobs for America as well. It's a good deal, and we ought to take it," crowed Bill Clinton at the signing of the North America free Trade Agreement.[34] "Now, as before, we will secure our nation, protect our freedom, and help others to find freedom of their own," proclaimed George Bush in the run up to the Iraq war.[35]

All opposition to the agenda of domination and control of resources is characterized as irrational—hidebound, narrow, and parochial. No wonder that reason and its vaunted universality have fallen into disrepute. Too many people have suffered at its hands. Too many have seen their communities torn apart, their wells poisoned, their livelihoods destroyed, their cultures trampled. They are left exposed and vulnerable. As their worlds disintegrate, they are integrated into the modern world, as fodder is "integrated" into the cow fattened for slaughter.

The progress of capital accumulation is proclaimed by those who reap the profits to be the progress of democracy, freedom, and human rights. But the benefits of freedom and democracy are enjoyed by only the narrowest stratum of privileged dwellers in the upper reaches of certain western societies. The pain imposed by those western societies has been felt in the vast reaches of Asia, Africa and Latin America, as well as in the ghettos and wretched backwaters of the world's richest nation. Beyond the narrow circle of "owners of the means of production" and their faithful flunkies all the talk of rights, democracy, and freedom is just so much chatter accompanying campaigns of plunder, pillage, and genocide. The world shaped by the irrational pursuit of profit is a world mercilessly divided between the exploited and the exploiters, a world in which the gap between rich and poor grows ever larger, a world of vast unnecessary misery, a world in which the very biological basis of life is threatened.

In the word of the exploited, all the promises of rights turn into their opposites: freedom entails enslavement; democracy, exploitation; inalienable rights, alienation of all rights. The rage against the false promises of those who claim they come to spread freedom and democracy is easily exploited by those who speak for God and wish to reestablish His—and their—authority. Rationality itself is a false god. The entire project of reason is discredited. All its fruits are lumped together—its science, its secular democratic values, its talk of inalienable rights and freedom, the vast globe swallowing institutions it has created, the entertainments in purveys. And all are turning rotten. We are urged to veil our women and our minds.

So should we defend reason, abandon it, or attempt to reclaim it? Has our faith in reason been misplaced? Should we leave unchallenged the System's claim to represent reason or should we challenge it in the name of a reason whose critical content is unimpaired? Is it possible to sever the link between the rationality of the System and its irrationality? Is there an

inextricable link between the virtues associated with rationality, and the vices that accompany it like camp followers?

* * *

The eighteenth century is called the Age of Reason (no one
would say the same for the twentieth or what we've seen so far
of the twenty-first). Back then, the project of reason was revolution. Reason was the source of values. The emerging middle
class used it as a weapon against the feudal nobility that
blocked the bourgeoisie's access to power. The reason of the
Enlightenment had a critical agenda: to challenge all authority
not founded in reason itself. It worked against the given. It led
to the beheading of a king and a queen, and the storming of
the Bastille. It fed the kerchunking blade of the guillotine.

The critique of the old order was based on the belief that
the equal rights of man had their foundation in nature. Locke,
Paine, and Jefferson derived the right to life, liberty, and property from natural law. Reason was the law of nature, and it
was also the mental faculty that enabled us to know that law.
"We hold these truths to be self-evident," wrote Jefferson in
our Declaration of Independence. By virtue of reason, nature's
law became "self-evident." The principles of a democratic
society were founded in nature as surely as the laws of physics
and astronomy. Access to truth was equally available to all.
Since reason was not the exclusive property of a privileged
class it was a fitting and necessary foundation for a democratic, secular, and egalitarian society.

The reason of merchants and accountants was, in this
period, wielded by the bourgeois against those classes and
institutions that stood in their way. Reason was a sword, bright
and clean to cut through ignorance, replacing the patriarchal
authority of kings and princes with the free will of a brood of

fatherless sons who chose to form an egalitarian fraternity of those who buy and sell. And if, in practice, there were those who were excluded from this fraternity—the propertyless rabble, women, paupers, slaves—the principles discovered by reason were at least, in theory, universal and capable of being used by those excluded to argue for their admission.

But that was then. What now? Feudalism has been overthrown. A social order designed for the benefit of merchants and shopkeepers is firmly entrenched. And the palace of the Sun King has been replaced by the gleaming skyscrapers of the new masters of the universe. Science has been their faithful servant, their fawning acolyte. Reason leveled the playing field only to provide the foundation for a new and more comprehensive hierarchy.

Reason has lost its bite. It has become a watchdog for the status quo, ferreting out inefficiency and disciplining the reprobate who does not directly contribute to the profit of its masters.

The failure of reason to rise to its critical task may help explain a curious phenomenon: One might have thought that by now, after many centuries of triumphs, reason would have cleared the world of gods, goblins, and spirits of the glen. Free at last, we should no longer be haunted by our fathers and mothers projected into the sky. "No Gods! No Masters!" cried Margaret Sanger and the Wobblies. Good riddance to the realm beyond appearances, where meaning and purpose is given to our meandering lives by invisible beings who create and intend the world. We should no longer require the services of priests, rabbis and mullahs, the anointed gatekeepers to the beyond, except occasionally for funerals and other special events.

But the opposite is the case. Secularism is on shaky ground these days.* Our elected officials may still occasionally claim that the values of democracy are founded in reason, but more often

* A 2007 Harris poll found that more people in the United States (62 percent) believe in the devil than in Darwin's theory of evolution (42 percent). Thirty-one percent believe in witches (http://www.reuters.com/article/lifestyleMolt/idUSN2922875820071129).

than not they forego the appeal to reason and head straight for
God, appealing to Him at every opportunity as if the Constitu-
tion had been handed down on Mt. Sinai, and Christ, crucified
on the cross, wrote the Bill of Rights "God told me to strike at
al Qaida and I struck them, and then he instructed me to strike
at Saddam, which I did, and now I am determined to solve the
problem in the Middle East," George Bush is reported to have
told Palesatinian Prime Minister Mahmoud Abbas.[36]

The gods are having a resurgence. As reason erodes the
foundation of belief, belief grows stronger. Rationality may
have undermined the prestige and power of the gods, but they
have not gone gently into that good night. "You still need us,"
they say through their spokespeople on earth, who take every
opportunity to warn us against the poison fruits of reason:
licentiousness, the loosening of restraints, and the destruction
of the moral order. Religion is still the heart of a heartless
world: a loving heart, an angry heart, a consoling heart.

Religions teach that there is a consciousness that created and
governs the world, an "objective" consciousness, independent
of our individual human subjectivity. Science has replaced a
world haunted by invisible spirits, with a world of hard facts
from which consciousness is excluded. Mind is locked in the
skull, like a prisoner in her cell, peering through the bars at a
world beyond her reach. She's let out only for the specific task
of prying open, breaking apart, reassembling, and ordering
things according to rules.

Scientists may be the freest of prisoners. They're released on
furlough, like poets and artists. Their minds are allowed to
wonder at will over the universe. The best are lovers of the
beauty of nature. They appreciate an elegant theory. The earth
viewed from space is an opalescent jewel. Peer through a tele-
scope and spiraling nebulae invisible to the naked eye swim
into view. Beauty inspires their curiosity. Their hypotheses may

come to them in dreams and reverie. But when the real work of science begins, the dreaming stops. The mind withdraws from the world, returns to its cell, and operates on the world from a distance. Just as the worker trudging to her job must leave her personal life behind, so the scientist must set aside what is essentially inaccessible to others—her personal experience of the world—when she enters the laboratory. The objectivity of science is obtained by peeling away what is unique and individual in experience, in order to get at what can be repeatedly verified. Scientists search in the bounty of nature for rules and regularities.

When all there is of reason is the objectivity of science and the neat bookkeeping of accountants, when science becomes the sum total, the pinnacle, and final expression of reason, then reason ceases to be, as it was in the eighteenth century, a source of values. It has nothing more to say about what matters most: about what ought to be, about justice, about loss, and pain, and love—the important things. It exhausts itself in facts and figures. Even though the world screams that something has gone terribly wrong, reason does not hear its cry. It turns a deaf ear.

The definitive separation of the world of objective fact from the world of subjectivity makes it difficult to discover a rational basis for value. Science, the golden child of reason, is very good at telling us what is, but abstains from comment on what ought to be. "Oughts" are not its business. Nor are they the business of the CEO, who is charged with maximizing the profits of his corporation's shareholders and pays lip service, as needed, to everything else. So who's in charge of values? If all there is of reason is science and accounting, and an empty logic, sterile as a hen without a rooster, where do values come from? Are we back to pointing to the sky? Do they float down from some transcendental realm like manna from heaven? Do they originate in an alternate universe? Do we make them up as we go along? Do they have a foundation that guarantees their universality or are they as individual and evanescent as snowflakes? If science rules only in the realm of what is, is the realm of ought-to-be, ruled by the irrational?

* * *

> *The System is a labyrinth large as the world, containing at its center a devouring monster. The monster is hideous and beautiful; it has the face of death and a body made for love. It has an enormous appetite. It is human and inhuman. It has many names—greed, profit, lust for power—but its secret name is unknown. The monster breaks our bones to get at the marrow, gobbles our hopes, sucks us dry of possibilities, reams out our imagination. It is insatiable. Brilliant minds hunched over their drawing boards, computers, and spreadsheets helped to create and continue to maintain the dwelling for this monster. The labyrinth is designed to confuse those who wish to slay the monster and lead them down false paths and blind alleys.*

Even when most deeply immersed in Motherfuckerism, I thought of reason as Ariadne's thread that we must follow if we are to emerge alive from the journey to the heart of the labyrinth. Without it, we would become lost and confused, imagining that we were heading out of the maze towards freedom, when in actual fact we were heading into the maw of the devouring beast.

But now I wonder: Is the reason that built the labyrinth, the same reason that we use as a thread to guide us out of it?

TRUTH WITH A CAPITAL T

SPEAKER FROM THE AUDIENCE: "There is after all something which is the truth which we can at least approach. . . . After all . . . Elvis Presley is either dead or he isn't." . . . I agree with you we can't get truth with a capital T back, but it seems to me there has to be some alternative short of a collapse into nihilism . . ."

WENDY BROWN: "I don't know how recognizing that Elvis Presley is probably more alive dead than he was when he was alive is nihilism . . . and I actually think to collapse those is again to resuscitate the accusation, that there is this thing called post-modernism which rejects all truth, it's all relativist, . . . it doesn't know its sitting on a chair, and it has no values . . . It's not the case that Elvis Presley is either dead or not dead. . . . I think it's a mistake . . . to make that move, to say that that is nihilism, and to rest your case on facticity."

—Exchange between member of the audience and Wendy Brown at forum on Left Conservatism, March 1998

The attack on reason's claim to universality and its right to have a say in determining what ought to be comes, not only from the proponents of revealed truth, but also from secular movements that claim there is no such thing as a single, unitary universal truth. Those movements all agree that reason, as primarily exemplified in the thinking of white men, is not Ariadne's thread. It's just a bit of yarn. She has many threads and they lead in many directions.

In 1992, Vaclav Havel, playwright and then president of Czechoslovakia, addressed a gathering of the world's most powerful politicians and CEO's at the World Economic Forum in Davos Switzerland, and pronounced the end of the reign "arrogant absolutist reason":

> The fall of Communism can be regarded as a sign that modern thought—based on the premise that the world is objectively knowable, and that the knowledge so obtained can be absolutely generalized—has come to a final crisis. This era has created the first global, or planetary, technical civilization, but it has reached the limit of its potential, the point beyond which the abyss begins. The end of Communism is a serious warning to all mankind. It is a signal that the era of arrogant, absolutist reason is drawing to a close and that it is high time to draw conclusions from that fact.[37]

Six years later, at the height of the academic fad for post-modernism and deconstruction, I attended a panel discussion at the University of California at Santa Cruz on "Left Conservativism." According to the organizers of the conference, left conservatives were believers in precisely the overarching, all-explaining theory founded in Marxism that Vaclav Havel condemned as the product of "arrogant, absolutist reason" and that I, growing up, thought of as the antidote to fascism.

The critics of Left Conservstivism said they did so in the name of "anti-foundationalism." What foundation were they against? No one bothered to explain. Was it substance as "foundation" to which attributes attach; the "self" as the "foundation" to which consciousness attaches; "the real" as the "foundation" of appearances; reality as the "foundation" for true statements about the world; reason as a "foundation" for argument; a material base as the "foundation" for a super-structure of ideas; all of these, or none? I had no idea.

Wendy Brown, one of the panelists and a professor of political science at the University of California, Berkeley, leveled a series of accusations against the left-conservatives. They had difficulty with anti-foundationalism's relentless questioning. They wanted their old "real" and "true" back. They wanted "truth with a capital "T." They mourned the loss of materiality. They were wedded to a belief in "the revolution," and "Marcuse's 'Great Refusal.'" They could not accept the "decentering of capitalism." They missed their old working class heroes, muscular and sweaty. She accused them of having nostalgia for Pete Seeger concerts. They needed someone to blame for the collapse of the left and anti-foundationalists were handy targets.

In the rather rancorous debate that followed the panel discussion, the so-called left conservatives in the audience denied that they still believed in the orthodoxies of Marxism—a strict economic determinism and a rigid division between material base and ideological superstructure. Somewhat to my surprise, they joined their anti-foundationalist opponents in disavowing a belief in "Truth with a capital T." What did that capital letter signify? Did it mean a truth that is universally true? If so why was everyone pledging allegiance to the lower case?

I rose to my feet, and walked over to where the microphone had been placed in an aisle on the opposite side of the lecture hall. I was trembling, my nervousness amplified by disability. I tried to stabilize myself by sitting on the arm of a chair, but my voice shook. When the microphone was lowered to accommodate me I managed to say that I am a believer in Truth with a capital T, all upper case, bold, and in neon lights. I went on to say, that there have been moments in political struggle, such as, for example, during the civil rights movement in the Sixties, when young Black men and women sat down in protest and were beaten, but refused to move. Those were the moments in which what is truly true and real is revealed and what passes for truth and reality is exposed as a lie and unreal. It is important, I continued, to expand those moments, and for theory to preserve and incorporate them into itself. And I am not sure that either anti-foundationalism or materialism could do that.

My speech was mercifully short, and largely drowned in the static of my quivering rebellious body. I felt thoroughly humiliated. I alone quivered and shook and betrayed my fear. I was a rank amateur among professionals. I was insufficiently familiar with the literature. So much to read. So much to remember. I experienced in full force the fear I experience in the philosophy sections of book stores, the fear of being wiped out by a gigantic wave of words, of drowning in an ocean of ideas. Truth be told, I have lived all my life without a foundation, quite certain that I could not justify with facts and figures and cogent argument, a fraction of my beliefs. I take them more or less on faith, glad that there are others, more competent than I to engage in debates and public controversy. Though I long for theory, I have done quite well without it, surviving on the remains of inherited coherence. And yet I believe firmly in a foundation, in the possibility, nay the necessity of universals, of the pursuit of coherence, and a version of reason and rationality that anti-foundationalism appears to question. I need truth with a capital T, a truth born in the promiscuous commingling of "is" and "ought."

I don't believe the world is changed by truths without capitals. (Of course, one can always be wrong. Truth with a capital "T" can turn out to be a mistake with a capital "M." It's a risk one takes—betting on the wrong horse.) How can we demand universal condemnation of injustice without at the same time demanding universal acknowledgement of the facts that constitute that injustice? We are certain that the African slave trade was an abomination because we can imagine what that trade meant for its victims. We want to hurl the facts of that trade in the face of anyone who would defend it. Feast your mind, we demand, on the middle passage: piss and vomit; darkness and iron shackles; branded skin; Black corpses thrown overboard, the sharks feasting, flesh rotting at the bottom of the ocean.

> Raphael painted, Luther preached, Corneille wrote, Milton sang; and through it all, for 400 year the sharks followed the scurrying ships; for 400 years America was strewn with the living and dying millions of a transplanted race; for 400 years Ethiopia stretched forth her hands unto God.[38]

Is this truth with a capital T? I think so.

In the lecture halls of universities, anti-foundationalists skirmish with left conservatives who still talk about the real, the true, the just, and persist in spinning a frayed Ariadne's thread of universals. Meanwhile, in the narrow streets of refugee camps and the plazas before mosques, synagogues and churches, fundamentalists mull their response to "arrogant absolutist reason" and catalogue the abominations of its camp followers. On the one side are those who deny the possibility of "truth with a capital T." On the other are those who believe they've got a franchise on it. Both fundamentalism and post-modernism are iatrogenic diseases that result from the radical separation of "ought" from "is." After surgery, a raging infection.

If "Truth with a capital T" is taken to imply some truth that stands outside of and utterly independent of history and time, eternal, unfiltered by consciousness, untouched by human hands, not subject to review or emendation, it's no wonder that both sides at the Santa Cruz conference give it a wide berth. Such truths belong to religion and revelation. They should be kept out of politics and science. What we do need are truths that are not just true for me or for you, truths that can be shared. We need truths with dimension and depth; truths that are pools in which we see ourselves reflected. We need:

Truths that tip toe quietly so as not to wake the children;

Truths that bray like a billy goat;

Truths that gush like sweat from the pores of marching miners;

Truths that erupt like spit from the mouths of angry shouters;

Truths that diffuse like a warm vapor from the whispering mouths of lovers;

Truths that penetrate like a dank smell of old latrines in the woods.

We need a world in common.

The System is a labyrinth large as the world.

THE COLOR OF REASON

I reject your theology, your history, your morality by which you don't live, your Gods and your standards and in total all of it, lock stock and barrel, because you don't live by them and I know that you don't live by them by the way you treat me.

—James Baldwin[39]

Five years before the end of the millennium, this country was in the grip of an obsession with the trials of Orenthal J. Simpson, an African-American former football player, sometime actor, and pitchman for Hertz Rent-A-Car, who was accused of murdering his estranged blond wife, Nicole Brown Simpson, and a White Jewish man, Ron Goldman, who apparently stopped by her house to return a pair of glasses. A predominantly Black jury acquitted Simpson in the criminal trial. A predominantly White jury found him liable in the civil trial that followed. Opinion polls showed that most Whites believed he had done it; most African-Americans that he had not. Both saw in the other's view an expression of racial bias. Neither thought the other was being objective.

Pundits expressed dismay at the racial divide this case revealed. They did not seem to notice that there was something on which both sides agreed: Either he did it or he didn't. There was a truth to be discovered. No one thought there were two alternate streams of reality, White and Black—in one of which OJ plunged the knife into Nicole and Ron, splattering their blood on his socks and glove, and another in which he was home practicing his golf swing at the time a person or persons unknown did the awful deed. The truth was hidden, but it was one. There was, however, no tribunal on which both sides could agree that could arbitrate what appeared to be a dispute between the races about what that single truth might be. Certainly it would not have worked to "appeal to reason." What reason? A White reason? A Black reason? A reason that transcended race?

* * *

In the Sixties, we spoke of "The Movement" as if it were a single entity, but in fact it was always divided along lines of race. In 1966, SNCC had embraced Black Power and decided to expel whites. It explained its decision in a position paper entitled "The Basis of Black Power":

> Negroes in this country have never been allowed to organize themselves because of white interference. As a result of this, the stereotype has been reinforced that blacks cannot organize themselves. The white psychology that blacks have to be watched, also reinforces this stereotype. Blacks, in fact, feel intimidated by the presence of whites, because of their knowledge of the power that whites have over their lives. One white person can come into a meeting of black people and change the complexion of that meeting . . . People would immediately start talking about brotherhood, love, etc.; race would not be discussed.[40]

The demand by people of color for recognition of the pervasiveness of racism and the demands by women for acknowledgement of sexism came as a shock to white men in the movement. We had been the heroes of our own fairy tale of revolution. Now others were writing a script in which we were cast in a less flattering light. We were used to being center stage. Now we were being told to move onto the wings. The solidarity we had imagined was largely a myth. The fault lines between oppressor and oppressed ran through the movement. The divisions ran deep and crisscrossed each other unexpectedly. The oppressed could also be the oppressor. What was the basis of unity? We no longer had the answers.

I had always believed that reason was universal. Its strictures applied to everyone. Its inclusiveness was a guarantee of human solidarity. It was the necessary foundation of that solidarity. If I had been asked, I would have said it transcended all divisions of race, class, and gender. It had not occurred to me that the reason to which I pledged allegiance could be seen as a project of mostly dead European white men, and that others might question its universality on that ground. The political movements to which I had given my allegiance were largely white. But after I left the Motherfuckers, people of color came to play an increasingly important role in my personal life. The man I loved most in my life, my best friend until he died of esophageal cancer, was Puerto Rican and Dominican. And my wife is African American. Neither of them let me rest in my unexamined assumptions about race.

* * *

I lie down next to Arisika. Her skin is luminous and soft. Its color varies with the light. I am white. My skin color also changes with the light. But though the color of our skin changes, the fact that Arisika is black and I am white does not. We cannot escape the social meaning of color. I am the color of the men who owned her ancestors. And sleeping with me, she sleeps with the enemy. I am also her lover, her husband, and her friend. We endeavor to make a separate peace.

I say "we endeavor," but this is not quite accurate. I have no sense of effort. Nothing we two can do together can erase the meaning of race in America. The recognition of the meaning of Arisika's color for white America is part of who she is, both for herself and for me. In my being with Arisika, color does not disappear. But as in speech, where the sounds of words become transparent with meaning, so, for me, Arisika's body is like a word soaked with the meaning of who she is for herself, and what she chooses to share with me. So full of these meanings is her body for me, that there is no room—or so I hope—for the defining gaze of the overseer.

* * *

For the racist, the consciousness of people of color is reduced to the corrupt effluvium of their bodies. Racism, in the crude form exemplified by the stereotype of the beer bellied Southern sheriff and hooded Klansmen, is easy to dismiss as irrational. But covert racism pervades the system. It insures that disproportionate numbers of African Americans will be consigned to the lowest rungs of the economic ladder. And the System still presents itself to the world as a rational enterprise.

No thought emanating from a society divided along lines of class, race, and gender can completely transcend those divisions. Reason, though aspiring to universality, in practice leaves those divisions intact. This "leaving intact," is reason's Achilles heel, as well as the necessary condition of all thought in an unfree society.

I keep wanting to shrug off this pessimistic assessment of the possibility of universality, and rush out to fill my lungs with the fresh air of reason, whose currents sweep unencumbered across the planet. I want to get on with the argument, offer a quick acknowledgement that bias is inevitable, and proceed. The Theory of Relativity, I protest, is not white, male, or Jewish. The same with Marxism and psychoanalysis. You can not judge the truth of an idea by its origin. The theory of relativity is ether true or false—for Blacks and Whites, Jews and Gentiles, bosses and workers. Marxism is not the same as fascism, though both are ideologies whose principal exponents have been white men. Even the statement that universality is suspect claims for itself universal applicability.

I am a white, six-foot-tall, bearded, partially disabled, middle-class Jewish American. I can imagine my writing characterized as white and male. I can not imagine it described as bearded or six feet tall. Thoughts do not have the same relation to the thinker that attributes have to objects. Objects are a particular color, so and so big across, such and such shape. If we could describe all their attributes, nothing would be left over. The ball is red. It can not escape its redness. But the "I" is always other than the thoughts it thinks. The thinker is not the thought. We are always one step ahead of ourselves.

Whiteness and masculinity are not physical characteristics of thought. Just as my writing is not an emanation of my beard, it is not an emanation of my white skin or male sexual organs. Whiteness and maleness are ideas and ideologies. The writing of white men will probably reflect these ideas and ideologies because white men are usually brought up in a white world and a patriarchal culture. A white man stolen at birth and brought up by wolves would have a different story to tell. In Europe, white male voices have risen up, time and again, on the side of the outcast, the downtrodden and exploited.

They have, on occasion, opposed ideologies of whiteness and maleness. And yet thought that stands in opposition can also betray its link to what it opposes. It may set itself against the prevailing forms of domination, but it cannot totally free itself from them. The thought of Marx and Freud, Voltaire and Jefferson, Socrates and Hegel is male, white, and European. And it is not. It is bounded and free.

Defenders of the achievements of European writers and thinkers insist that the truths they have discovered are universal. They often rail against anyone who questions that universality and exposes its unsavory underpinnings. On the other hand, those who do not find their truth reflected in the European canon, those who find themselves cast out, disparaged, and rendered invisible, at times deny altogether that any truth is universal and end up labeling thought as one would produce in a market: white thought in this bin; male thinking in that. And in the next aisle over—Black science and women's rationality.

* * *

Reason is not Black or White, male or female. This principle lies at the foundation of everything I believe. You cannot pry my fingers loose from it. It's my life raft. The fact that Thomas Jefferson was a slave owner links the Declaration of Independence to white racism. But it does not mean that the idea that we all have a right to life, liberty, and the pursuit of happiness is a white idea. Its whiteness consists in its fluid accommodation to the institution of slavery, and all subsequent inequalities. It is white in so far as it has permitted and facilitated that accommodation.

* * *

It's no wonder that those who have suffered under a system that treats them as things—all the while laying claim to rationality and universality—become wary of claims made in the name of reason and come to distrust high sounding talk about "equality" and our common "essential humanity."

We do not encounter "essential humanity" walking down the street, waiting at a bus stop, or standing ahead of us at the checkout counter. We encounter particular humans of varying shapes, sizes, genders, colors, and proclivities. There are myriad differences between us, myriad ways in which we are not equal, but we are told they are irrelevant. They are contingencies, unconnected to our essential humanity. They fall outside the net.

The process of abstraction by which liberal theory distills a common humanity does not require us to actually come together to resolve our differences. It sweeps us together in theory, but not in practice. It does not demand that we organize society in a way that insures the convergence of our interests. The System wants to have it both ways. It declares us all equal under the skin, and uses our skin as a marker for sorting those who are treated as humans and those who are not. It is dependent for its very existence on the perpetuation of gross inequalities. It can produce a steady crop of Clarence Thomases, Colin Powells, and Condoleezza Rices. A Barack Hussein Obama can be president of the United States! It does not tremble when Black and White people have sex together, when women have sex with women, and men with men, despite the squeals of prurient dismay arising from certain quarters. In the South, the descendants of slaves and the descendants of slave masters pee in the same toilets, after a huge struggle. But it still remains the case that in the global gradient of wealth and power, the poorest people are the darkest, and in no country—including the United States—are the lighter skinned people, as a whole, poorer than the darker.

Women and people of color are still buffeted by howling gales of malice that strip them of their dignity, their dreams, their agency, and their very lives. They cannot ride out the storm by clinging to the hope that the storm will abate as soon as their "essential humanity" is recognized. And so, born into a sea of troubles, they construct life-raft identities from the debris that has been cast aside to obtain the concept "human." They form identities from all those traits, which they are told by liberal theory are meaningless and irrelevant, but which they have found are precisely the traits on which the system has inscribed their fate.

We tend to think of identity as something concrete, whole, and unmediated—the opposite of what is universal and abstract. But while the concepts "woman," or "African-American" are less inclusive than the concept "human being," they remain concepts. By proclaiming the importance of their identity, women and African Americans are not taking the side of being against thought. They think themselves in opposition to the System. They enter into a battle, which is, among other things, a battle of ideas. They demand recognition of the ways in which their gender and skin color have determined their history, and shaped their consciousness.

A multiracial/multigendered global corporate hegemony would still be a disaster, despoiling the planet, sickening us, breeding misery and starvation in the midst of plenty. It would still be a hideous irrationality. But the system is not blind to color or gender. It is built on preexisting foundations of white supremacy and patriarchy. As Christians built their churches on the foundations of pagan temples, so capitalism has built its structure of class division on foundations of race and gender exploitation. It has taken the stones of those old structures and incorporated them into the walls of the temple of Mammon. The domination of women by men goes back to the beginning of recorded history. The large scale exploitation of people of African descent begins in the fifteenth century with the European slave trade. These primitive modes of domination have not disappeared in the development of capitalism. They are integrated into its structure at the deepest level. While it would appear at first glance that capitalism could organize itself quite well on the basis of race and gender equality, hierarchies of race and gender persist with only minimally diminished virulence. They provide a rationale for super-exploitation, and serve to mask the fundamental class structure of capitalist exploitation. In the dust stirred up by conflicts about race and gender, that structure disappears from view, just as fish beneath the water disappear when the surface is turbulent.

The extent to which hierarchies of race and gender will remain if the class structure of capitalism is abolished cannot be known until we have completed the process of dismantling those structures. Until we pull at the system we will not know how it comes apart. But this much we do know: The system is a totality. And an effective challenge to it must be a total challenge.

The unity necessary for such a challenge cannot be reached by impatiently brushing aside concerns about race, gender, and identity. That is to say, it cannot be reached over the bodies of those who feel turned to stone by the institutionalized gaze of patriarchy and white supremacy. To dismiss their concerns is to indulge in the kind of abstraction which the system has made suspect. We cannot get to the universal by bracketing gender and race and setting it aside. The universal only manifests itself through the particular. Our myriad histories and endlessly varied bodies are the medium through which, and only through which, our common humanity emerges. This common humanity exists inextricably bonded to our diversity.

* * *

We can embrace diversity without giving in to a distrust of all abstraction and claims to universality. Distrust of universalizing reason is understandable. We long for connection, for a place on the earth where we feel we belong. We long for family and community. We long for roots, for tribal ways, for the world as it was when the concrete and the particular were not threatened by the giant anonymous engines of rationality and abstraction. The train those engines drive seems increasingly headed for disaster.

The irrationalities of the System, which claims to be the embodiment of rationality cannot be attributed solely to a problem of implementation—shoddy execution of the master plan. The fact that the theory of relativity leads in practice to the possibility of nuclear holocaust does not make it wrong, anymore than the fact that Nazis counted off their victims makes arithmetic wrong. But it does speak to the inadequacy of a reason that is limited to science and mathematics, and to the need for a larger horizon for rationality.

When the distrust of the rationality of the system leads to a distrust of all thought that moves towards the universal by way of abstraction, then our ability to think together a way out of the labyrinth is put in jeopardy. For in order to flush the system out of hiding and prevent its constant shape-shifting, we must find a way to hold it in thought so that we can grasp it in fact and tear it apart.

AND THE MINOTAUR MOOED

I believed as a child that the path marked out by reason was the path humanity must follow to achieve true happiness. I thought of reason as a kind of slow pleasure, a clean burning fuel, which would leave no unpleasant residue and would last a lifetime. Fill your tank with reason. Abjure the fast dirty pleasures of sex and the body, or at the very least, indulge in moderation and discreetly—those were the commandments I internalized. If I could but follow those commandments! My failure caused me shame and guilt. Alone in my bedroom I masturbated and indulged in sadomasochistic fantasies, while in his study Herbert was writing *Eros and Civilization*, arguing with Freud about *Civilization and Its Discontents*, and the relation between reason and happiness. Much is at stake in that argument. If the marriage between reason and happiness is annulled, we will take the side of happiness every time.

* * *

In my parents' home I imbibed the mother's milk of Marxism. I thought if I drank deeply enough my mind would open to the grand design woven into the fabric of history. But I stopped my intellectual breastfeeding too early and spent more time than was good for me reading Dostoevsky. Franz's Marxism was of the social democratic variety. Before fleeing

Germany he had been a prominent labor lawyer, and there was always something lawyerlike and precise about his thinking. It was brilliant, but it had little appeal to me.

Herbert, on the other hand, has been a lasting influence. The guiding principle of his thought is "the dialectic," a logic that embraces contradiction as its guiding principle. Contradiction is not to be avoided. Reality is contradictory, and thought that hopes to grasp reality must embrace contradiction. The dialectic is a dance of being and thought to the rhythm of becoming and passing away. In the dance of the dialectic, idea and reality are intricately intertwined. Arm in arm they move across the dance floor, one, yet separate. Dancing the dance of the dialectic, the world and thought move forward through time and towards truth. Every doing is an undoing, every birth a funeral, every marriage a divorce. Each historical period generates within itself the forces that will crack it open, just as the egg incubates the chick that in due time will break the shell that imprisons it. Those who dance on the grave of the old order fulfill its promise. The dialectic is a tango of struggling combatants: what-will-be wars with and embraces what-is.

People in America don't do the dialectic. It's a European dance form. Herbert and his colleagues of the Frankfort school carried its secret steps across the ocean into exile. The dialectic was nothing, mere thought pitted against the Nazi war machine. But it seemed to me that woven into its steps was Ariadne's thread, the clue to the maze, and therefore the key to the ultimate triumph over fascism. Very early in life, children pick up certain habits of mind from the adults with whom they live. As a young Waadabi boy might watch the dancing of his elders to learn the tribe's traditional steps and rhythms, so did I watch the intellectual dance of my parents to learn the proper movements of the mind.

It is difficult for me in retrospect to decide whether or not the version of Marxism I grew up with included a belief in the inevitable triumph of what-ought-to-be. Was it inevitable that the System would fall apart from its own internal contradictions, and burst open like a piece of rotten fruit? Was the triumph of the proletariat—that class which was chosen by history as the designated agent of truth, and the custodian of denied possibilities—preordained? Perhaps the grownups themselves were not sure on this point.

Merely to say that something is possible is not to say it "ought" to be. Nor does saying that something ought to be imply its possibility. That something ought to be is not very interesting unless, at the same time, we can show that it is not merely a nice idea, or even a possibility in the sense that anything is possible, but a "real" possibility, an ought imprisoned within the "is," an ought that is the truth of the "is."

Marxism is not concerned with any "ought," but this. It doesn't moralize. The ought is the real in chains. Those chains can only be broken when the time is ripe. But time does not ripen by itself. It ripens through work, energy, and imagination. The fabric of history is never off the loom. The weaver learns the pattern from the weaving. The fabric weaves the weaver as surely as it is woven by her. So how can anything be inevitable?

The birth canal of what-is-to-be passes through the pelvis of human thought. The future is born in the painful contractions of consciousness, where nothing is inevitable even in the midst of the most dire necessity. Historians busy themselves with drawing up of a ledger of causes that purport to be sufficient to explain why history took the path it did. But their ledger is never complete. To say that something had to happen is to add nothing to the statement that it did happen. Inevitability is always retrospective.

* * *

I have a close friend, Alan, who is a doctor. His father, a phys-
iologist, was the director of the Woods Hole Marine Biological
Laboratory on Cape Cod. Alan grew up surrounded by scientists as I grew up surrounded by philosophers. He spent hours
in his father's laboratories, playing with colored chalk on the
blackboard, and as he grew older, helping with experiments.
He combed the beaches, sometimes alone, sometimes accompanied by his dad, picking up horseshoe crabs, starfish, and
jellyfish. He probed dead birds with a stick. He caught fish and
dissected them. He swam and rowed in Buzzard's Bay. His
childhood was filled with light: the light pouring in through
the windows of his father's laboratory; the bright sunlight of
beaches, dunes, and harbors; the clear and perfect light that
Edward Hopper captured on the white walls of Cape Cod
lighthouses, and the white sails of boats in the bay.

Alan's father did research on the transfer of fluids through cell
membranes. Frogs were his favorite experimental animals. In
shades of green and brown they sat stoically in the corners of his
laboratory waiting their turn to give their lives to science. Their
throats were the only things that moved. Alan remembers helping with an elegant experiment to prove the ability of their skin
to extract the amount of salt they need to survive from the fresh
water ponds and lakes which are their natural environment. He
peeled the skin from the hind leg of a frog, and fashioned out of
it a small pouch. The skin remained alive. This was essential for
the success of the experiment. He sewed the pouch shut at the
knee and the ankle and then immersed it in saline solutions of
varying concentration. After a time, the pouch would begin to
fill with fluid. When he measured the salt content of the fluid
inside the pouch he discovered that it remained remarkably constant, despite the variations in the saltiness of the water outside.

Not only that, but the amount of salt in the fluid was consistent with that to be found in the tissue of living frogs.

Alan learned in the way that children learn such things, that in brine and bone there was beauty and order, a pattern within the flux. To be an adult was to know that order and have access to that beauty. As I knew that I was born to be a professor, preferably of philosophy, so Alan knew he was destined to be a scientist. While I veered off track into Motherfuckerism, he remained true to his calling, and became a professor of neurobiology at Berkeley before dropping out and bringing his wife and children to live with us at Black Bear. After Black Bear we both dropped back in. I went to law school, he to medical school.

My friend now lives in a house on a cliff overlooking the Pacific Ocean. He takes his grandchildren on walks along the beach and encourages their interest in birds and beasts and all things natural, just as his father had done with him.

My friend and I grew up with different versions of reason. His was not murky. It did not contend with death camps and storm troopers, nor did it countenance the promiscuous commingling of "ought" and "is." His science was clear and bright and clean. The wonderful correspondence between, for example, the Fibonacci sequence of number and the spirals of a nautilus shell, between the order of thought and the order of the world, became visible only when the salt of subjectivity had been drawn from the mind by the filtering membrane of scientific method. On one side of that membrane sparkled a clear pool of objectivity; on the other, oughts and shoulds formed a brackish puddle of pond-scum that had no place in a well run laboratory.

In the laboratories of Alan's childhood, fish swam in tanks, frogs sat meditating in terrariums, bones rested on shelves, glass tubes, slides, and microscopes were kept free from dust in cabinets. Thought was about things that the eye could see

The cry of newborn hopes sounded in the gloom of unspeakable events.

and the hand could touch. In my fathers' studies there were books. Floor to ceiling. Row upon row of them. Books bound in cloth and leather. Books in Latin, Greek, German, French, and English. They smelled of cigarette smoke and held ideas. I learned that it was only through ideas that one touched the world, never directly. And the world my fathers had ideas about was first and foremost an historical world with nature as its background; a world filled with the smoke of battlefields, the groans of the wounded, the clamor of the marketplace, and the jubilation of revolutionaries celebrating their short lived triumphs. The cry of newborn hope sounded in the gloom of unspeakable events, and the light illuminating those events filtered through an uncertain thicket where what ought-to-be is forever caught in the brambles of what is.

* * *

I thought of my fathers' books as a vast treasure of theory, dug from the soil of daily life and accumulated over centuries by humanity in its struggle to understand itself. Thought slumbered in those books, breathing softly like a hibernating bear, waiting to be awakened by the warm attentions of a reader. Franz retreated to his study from my mother's dissatisfaction. Surrounded by his books, he would sit on the couch, smoke, and do the *New York Times* crossword puzzle. I would look in on him and wonder whether I too, would seek the sanctuary of theory when I reached my manhood. Would I inherit his treasure?

I would not. I left home and ran from theory into action, first to the wordless mimicry of painting, then to Motherfuckering on the streets of the Lower East Side, and later still to country life in the fir forests of Northern California. At

Black Bear, snowed in in the winter and running naked in the summer, I milked goats in the darkness of an old wooden barn that smelled like the inside of an animal. The goats shifted from foot to foot on the milking stand. They allowed my hands to squeeze their warm udders. Their milk pinged on the bottom of the pail. They never said a word. I assumed that somewhere else someone was taking care of theory. It didn't need me. Others would milk life for its meaning better than I ever could.

✻ ✻ ✻

When I have sought in the world for a body of thought as bright, light footed, and compelling as the one I imagined my fathers brought over from Europe, I have generally been disappointed. Perhaps no such theory exists or has ever existed.

I remember one day when I was still in high school in the Bronx, I found a flier lying on the sidewalk outside the subway stop at 242nd Street and Broadway. It was an invitation to attend a lecture on dialectical theory sponsored by some obscure socialist party whose name I have long since forgotten. I was anxious to find in the world some echo of the ideas discussed at my parents' table, so I stuffed it in my pocket, and on the appointed evening took myself to the address it listed, which turned out to be an undistinguished warehouse building. I followed the signs up the steps to a large barren loft. The walls were the color of old oatmeal. Hung here and there were portraits of Marx, Engels, and Trotsky, and posters in red and black of workers in heroic poses. At one end of the room was a table behind which the lecturer sat reviewing his notes. Facing him were rows of wooden folding chairs, mostly empty. There were about thirty people in the audience, all older than myself by far, all men. I remember them as stooped and gray-ing, and dressed in shabby wrinkled clothing. A number of them turned and smiled at me encouragingly as I took my seat in the back.

The lecture began. The speaker produced a large chart that he propped on an easel next to the desk. The chart depicted the stages of history beginning at the bottom with the age of dinosaurs and ending at the top with the triumph of commu-nism. Dialectical theory, the speaker explained, revealed the driving forces behind all history. Each thing that is, contains what will be within itself as its contradiction. Each stage of history develops within itself forces that will become irrecon-cilable, bringing on a crisis which will be simultaneously its death throws and the birth pangs of a new age. A new syn-thesis will emerge and at the same time new contractions, and so on. As mammals that scampered beneath the feet of dinosaurs, timid and unremarked, in time supplanted the dimwitted reptilian rulers of the savannahs, so the merchant class, trading in the shadow of the palaces of feudal lords, would in due course seize the reins of state and behead the monarchs of the old order. In this manner history progresses from epoch to epoch. The future now belongs to the working class whose mission it is to destroy the world order of capi-talism and whose victory will introduce the final stage of history, the abolition of classes, and the worker's paradise.

The lecturer explained the dialectic by offering as an exam-ple the growth of plants. The seed gives way to the seedling, the flower to the fruit, each later stage being the fulfillment of the former, and its destruction.* I tried to follow his analogy

* The metaphor is filched from Hegel: "The bud disappears in the bursting-forth of the blossom, and one might say that the former is refuted by the latter; similarly when the fruit appears, the blossom is show up in its turn as a false manifestation of the plant, and the fruit now emerges as the truth of it instead."(Hegel, *Phenomenology of Spirit*, translated by A. V. Miller (Oxford: Oxford University Press, 1977), p. 2.)

but it was hard for me to see the great struggles of history—workers building barricades, tearing up cobblestones for ammunition, troops laying down a withering hale of gunfire to disperse the demonstration—in the mute unfolding life of plants. I became distracted. An image of a potted geranium popped into my head. It was starved for water and sunlight. It sat root-bound in its clay pot on the windowsill of a dark loft. Poor plant. I felt sorry for it—and for me.

As the speaker wound towards his conclusion, I tried to pay attention, but succumbed to a deep weariness and lost track. Why, I thought, if they know so much, are there only thirty old men and me in this musty lecture hall? Why is it that no one cares? Or listens? What use is this truth, so large and unwieldy, smelling of dust and old newspapers? I left and never returned, despite my promises to the kind gentlemen who thanked me profusely for coming and reminded me of the dates of future presentations.

* * *

In Tony Kushner's *Slavs!*, Aleksii Antedilluivianovich Prelapsarianov, "the world's oldest Bolshevik" seeing the hopes of the Russian revolution shattered as a dream is shattered by the jangling of an alarm clock, bemoans the loss of a "theory." He wishes for a theory as Archimedes wished for a platform, from which he could move the world.

> "[S]how me the Theory," he cries, "and I will be at the barricades, show me the next Beautiful Theory, and I promise you these blind eyes will see again just to read it, to devour that text. Show me the words that will reorder the world, or else keep silent."[41]

As a child, I imagined Marxism to be a theory that could "reorder the world." It was the crowning achievement of reason, the culmination of its long struggle with lies and illusion. Reason's aspirations to universality matched those of the System itself. It taught that, just as all commodities have in common their monetary value, so all workers have in common their fundamental condition of wage slavery. The process of abstraction and exploitation that creates generic monetary value for the capitalist also creates "the worker," the universal, generic, source of wealth. The working class is that class, which, by struggling in its own interest, struggles in all our interest. The pursuit of its class interest would lead to the abolition of classes.

It is a grand vision, but it no longer captures the imagination of the "masses" as it once did. Where are the "masses"? They've dried up like puddles in the summer sun. The heroic "worker" has gone with them. People have multiple identities. "Worker" is only one, and it's not necessarily privileged over the others. Marxism, we are told, has been "discredited" by the historical failure of its predictions. Capitalism has not collapsed under the weight of its contradictions. On the contrary, Russia, the worker's paradise, has fallen into ruins, exposing for all to see gulags of filth, brutality, and corruption. Marxism, we hardly knew you, and now we miss you.

The Soviet Union is gone and so is theory. Fundamentalists of all stripes, post-modernists, anti-foundationalists, and deconstructionists, as well as many whose resistance to the System is based on racial or gender identity, have proclaimed the end of "arrogant absolutist reason"—may she rest in peace. Proclaim they may, but it still remains the case that the most profound challenges to the System have come from movements of social change which have at their heart a rationality that is not arrogant, a rationality that has something to say about what ought to be.

The Southern civil rights movement took on an entrenched system of segregation and white supremacy. Bus boycotts, marches, and sit-ins exposed that system as unjust and irrational. The System revealed its true nature in its response to those that challenged it: in the murder of civil rights workers, the bombing of churches, and the clubbing of non-violent demonstrators. The truth revealed itself in shared struggle. It revealed itself not to an "I" but to a "we"—the "beloved community" generated in that struggle. The true nature of the System came into view at the moment it ceased to be accepted as necessary and inevitable. At that moment it revealed itself as contingent and vulnerable because it was built on false foundations.

A rationality that considered values beyond its scope and confined itself to the manipulation of concepts and things would have been utterly alien to the thinking of the civil rights movement. The pursuit of justice and the exposure of irrationality were linked. Their common goal was freedom.

Freedom! The word expands like a flower, like the succulent prickly bud of an artichoke. It reminds us of intimate longings whose names we have forgotten, and collective grief we've come to take for granted. It links the language of law to the language of the heart. It links the practical to the utopian, the personal to the political, earthly struggles to dreams of flying. Its demands are eminently reasonable and they transcend reason, for the ultimate aim of freedom is to romp in the sweet by and by, to throw off every fetter, to cast aside all the clothing of inhibition. And who in the midst of orgasm thinks of rationality in any of its forms? Reason as the foreplay of pleasure? Perhaps.

The rhetoric of the Southern civil rights movement combined, in peculiar amalgam, biblical images of release—release of the soul from its mortal coils, release of the children of

Israel from bondage in Egypt—with a passionate argument for equal rights under the law. The movement demanded the familiar rights of liberal democracy, with a fervor born of the conviction that "there's a better world awaiting." This world—with its lynchings and bombings, with its "Bull" Conners and all their clubs and snarling dogs and fire hoses—will fade in the light of freedom, and give way under the weight of its injustice. The present is a chain upon a future ready to be born. The "better world awaiting" will be more real and true and good than this one.

The Southern civil rights movement demanded equality and clothed that demand in the rhetoric of revelation. As resistance to this simple demand hardened it became clear that the achievement of real equality would require the structural transformation of society. The link the Southern Civil rights movement forged between the fulfillment of the simple promises of reason, the larger systemic transformation of society, and a dream of liberation, set the pattern for the movements that have followed.

In their own way, all the various, disparate and contradictory strands of Sixties movements were fueled by the imagination of a "better world awaiting." Dropouts voyaging to another reality through doors of perception unlocked by LSD; students demanding the end to the war; Motherfuckers railing at Bill Graham; Black Panthers in black berets demanding Black Power; each, in their own and overlapping ways, endeavored to "break on through to the other side." Each had a vision of transcendence, of a comprehensive and all-inclusive reversal of fortune. The systemic transformation they envisaged would be a double unveiling. First the System's mask of benevolence would be torn away, its hidden violence exposed, the nakedness of power revealed, rampant beneath the skirts of civility. Then the naked reality behind the mask would be shown, in turn, to be another untruth, hiding the reality of deferred possibilities. This double unveiling could take place only through struggle.

The truth, we were clear, does not emerge in thought alone, but only in the process by which the world is changed into a more truthful state, a world in which truth no longer hides, appearances reflect reality, and surfaces reveal the depths beneath them.

* * *

Reality is revealed in the effort to realize an idea. Fight for freedom and justice and you'll see what the world is really like. Conversely, the truth of the idea is revealed in the process of its realization. Until we speak our thoughts or write them down, they shape-shift in our head. The thought of a beautiful painting is a ghost until the artist picks up her brushes and puts forms and colors on the canvas. The idea of the Cuban revolution was merely an untested dream until the voyage of the *Granma* and the trek into the Sierra Maestra.

If the truth of an idea is revealed in the process of its realization, then reason, whose goal is truth, must have a part in that process of realization. "Philosophers have only interpreted the world in various ways; the point, however, is to change it." Marx's admonishment is not a summons to retreat from interpretation and understanding, but a reminder that the process of discovering the truth and changing the world are intimately related and inseparable.

Philosophical issues are political. If we live inside a lie, if self and not-self, appearance and reality, universal and particular fall apart, that falling apart reflects a particular historical condition. Ultimately the restoration of the contradictory unity/disunity that defines the relation of consciousness to reality awaits the revolution. Revolution alone will bring thought home to the world. Till then, any image reason has of itself, will be incomplete, provisional, and subject to radical revision, for it will be the product of mere thought, locked within itself, untried and untested. And if the revolution must be permanent and will never be completed once and for all, then it would seem also that reason will never fully know itself.

Ariadne's thread was a guideline that Theseus unspooled behind him when he entered the labyrinth, and which he followed out when he left. But in the maze of time we can not leave the way we came. The path in is never the path out. The way to liberation is unexplored territory. The labyrinth and the path to freedom arise in time, moment by historical moment. Only what is past is fixed, and we can not tell by looking backwards where we should go, and therefore whether the thread we have followed does in fact lead out of the maze or deeper into it. And the thread that leads out now, may, in the future, become a chain holding us back. It may weave us into the wall of the labyrinth from which we seek to escape.

From this complexity, reason tells me, there is no escape. Except in dreams.

* * *

Tired of my doubts and questions, I fell asleep and dreamt that Ariadne and Theseus lay down in one of the corridors of the maze and made love. And the Minotaur mooed and produced milk, and the walls became transparent. Ariadne's thread was no longer needed. It became a snake, and shed its skin. And reason was reborn as the logic of desire,

*and the form of feeling. As slaves cast off the
names imposed upon them by their masters, so
reason at that moment took another name. But
when I awoke, I could not remember what it was.*

And the Minotaur mooed.

NOTES

1. Letter from Karl Marx to Arnold Ruge, September 1843, http://www.marx-ists.org/archive/marx/works/1843/letters/43_09.htm.
2. "The United Front Song," *Songs of the Spanish Civil War*, words by Bertolt Brecht, music by Kurt Weill, The Socialist Songbook, p.31, http://hengstrom.net/songbook/31.html.
3. H. Stuart Hughes, *The Sea Change: The Migration of Social Thought 1930-1965*, Harper and Row, 1975.
4. Feodor Dostoevsky, "Notes from the Underground," *White Nights and Other Stories*, The (New York: MacMillan Company, 1918) p. 54, Electronic Text Center, University of Virginia Library, http://etext.virginia.edu/etcbin/ toccer-new2?id=Dos-Note.sgm&images=images/modeng&data=/texts/english/modeng/parsed&tag=public&part=2&division=div2.
5. Joyce Milton, "The Times Are A-Changin' at Swarthmore," May 18, 2004, Front-PageMagazine.com, http://www.frontpagemag.com/Articles/Printable.asp?ID=13361; Elizabeth Weber, "The Crisis of 1969," March 7, 1996, *The Phoenix*,
6. Leroi Jones and Amiri Baraka, "Black People!" *The Leroi Jones/Amiri Baraka Reader*, edited by William J. Harris (New York: Thunder's Mouth Press, 1991), p. 224.
7. The poem was written by Rex Weiner, who went on to become a writer for movies and television, including *Miami Vice*. He writes in an email:

> Thirty-nine years ago an eighteen year old poet walked into the Tenth Street storefront office of Up Against The Wall Mother-fucker and handed you his first poem. It began with the line: "When the angry body moves through battlefield streets…" The short poem was inspired by the processions that erupted spon-taneously from the UAW/MF headquarters, street people banging garbage can lids, winos waving bottle of Thunderbird, snarling traffic, confounding the cops. The events kindled a glo-rious fever of rebellion in those who joined in and also a kind of apocalyptic fever … "Beep beep, bang bang, ungawa, fire power …"

I was the young poet. Drunk on Ginsberg and Mayakovsky, the Fugs and Woody Guthrie, I was thrilled to hang out in that place, listening to the endless and often hilarious meetings led by you and Ben Morea. It all seemed so smart and dangerous. I'd come from a stifling small north Westchester town, escaping by finishing high school in three years and getting admitted to NYU. I'd hitchhiked to San Francisco the summer of 1967 and caught hepatitis on a Big Sur commune—had to postpone my entry to NYU to the second semester. Got a pad that winter on Avenue B between 12th and 13th and stumbled through the garbage strike into the UAW/MF office.

There was one march to the 10th precinct down on 5th Street where we were demanding the release of someone named Henry. Every kept chanting "Henry . . . Henry . . . Henry!" Someone scaled the façade of the precinct building even as Capt. Fink came out to try to calm the crowd. "Who is Henry?" he asked. "I'm Henry" replied everyone in the crowd. Suddenly Fink noticed the guy clinging to the wall about twenty feet up. "Hey—what are you doing? Come down from there!" he hollered. "It's Henry!" someone yelled. "Henry . . . Henry . . . Henry!"

Adhering to revolutionary principles, I abandoned my ego and signed the poem Henry. It seemed like the right thing to do. When it came off the press in the back of the office on yellow paper superimposed ominously on a huge black fly, the poem was signed "Henry." I was very pleased and proud. It was the first thing I'd ever had published that expressed something of what I was feeling, what I was about.

Actually Henry was not a person. "Henry," is what we called our protests/demonstration/riots in the hope of confusing the police. We'd call for "a Henry tonight" and people knew that meant come to the corner of St. Mark's Place and 2nd Avenue ready to rumble. As far as I know, there never was any particular Henry who inspired the name.

8. John McMillan, *"Revolution by Theater" Remapping New Left History at the Battle of the Pentagon,* unpublished thesis.

9. Jerry L. Avorn and members of the staff of the Columbia Daily Spectator, *Up Against the Ivy Wall: A history of the Columbia crisis* (New York: Atheneum, 1969), p. 25-27.

10. Mark Rudd "Symbols of the Revolution," *Up Against the Ivy Wall: A history of the Columbia crisis,* Ibid., p. 291.

11. Mark Motherfucker recalls helping to fight off some football players who tried to invade Hamilton late the first night and being told afterwards by one of the

men he had been helping: "I've got the Black Panthers, and I've got SNCC and we're upstairs and we've got M1's. Are you ready for this? You look like you're ready." He spent the rest of the night pondering the question and deciding he was. But apparently the black students decided they weren't. The next day the guns got taken out. About ten young black men, dressed like members of a band in green pants and red shirts, came to the building. They were carrying saxophone cases, guitar cases, trombone cases, base cases, and guitar cases. They were in the building for about an hour. When they left, the guns left with them, concealed in the instrument cases (Author's interview with Mark, December, 2003). Tom Hurwitz on the other hand remember someone carrying the rifles out in a duffle bag and Julius Lester walking out "with a suitcase full of gray metal."

12. *Up Against the Ivy Wall: a History of the Columbia Crisis,* Ibid., p. 64-65.

13. From the author's Interview with Mark Motherfucker, recorded December 3, 2003.

14. John Motherfucker, "Math's Final Battle." Unpublished reminiscence emailed to the author April 8, 2008.

15. See http://lists.village.virginia.edu/sixties/HTML_docs/Resources/Primary/Manifestos/SDS_Port_Huron.html.

16. Quoted in Marilyn Bardsley, "Confession," *Charles Manson,* http://www.crimelibrary.com/serial_killers/notorious/manson/confess_4.html.

17. Document disclosed pursuant to a settlement in *Handschu v. Special Services,* a class action law suit against the New York Police Department spying on political groups. The case was filed in 1971 and settled in 1985.

18. Graham may have had more reason for seeing us as Nazi's than I recall. According to John Glatt "The fuse [for Graham's conflict with the Motherfuckers] was lit by the underground community newspaper the *East Village Other,* which became his tenants when he bought the Fillmore East. Soon afterward, the paper attacked Graham cruelly, saying it was a pity that he hadn't followed his parents into the Nazi concentration camps. Graham unexploded and stormed into the paper's office, tipped [?] over the editor's desk and threw him out into the street." (John Glatt, *Rage and Roll, Bill Graham and the Selling of Rock* Birch Lane Press Book, Published by Carol Publishing Group, pp 110-11; see also Bill Graham and Robert Greenfield, *Bill Graham Presents, My Life in Rock and Roll,* Doubleday 1992, pp. 253-254). Bill incorrectly implies it was the Motherfuckers who wrote an article in which we said it was "a shame" he didn't go with his parents into the camps.(*Id.* at 254.) Bill's description of our initial contact is far more benign than any of us recall:

> Some people came in Tuesday night and asked they could speak to me about a project involving the street merchants and representatives of all the different Lower at East Side organizations. One of them was called the Motherfuckers, a sociopolitical

street gang. They wanted their own night at the Fillmore to "express themselves." They said "You know, Bill, you always say you are part of the community, man. *Prove it.*"

I said, "Fine. Every Wednesday night is yours. You respect the building and will operate in. You can use it that night but only under our jurisdiction."

19. Richard Goldstein, "The Theater of Cruelty comes to Second Avenue," *The Village Voice,* October 31, 1968, p. 46-47; Lita Elisen, "Up Against the Wall, Bill Graham," *East Village Other,* October 25, 1968, p. 9; Paul Nelson, "The Motherfuckers, Fillmore East vs. The East Village: The Full Report," *Rolling Stone,* February 15, 1969, p. 6.

   Glatt's version is that when one of the actors announced the people were going to liberate the Fillmore it "immediately provoked Graham to leap from his seat and dashed on stage to defend his Fillmore against attack. Quickly overpowered, Graham was tied to a chair on the stage, where he remained for nearly six hours, arguing and screaming at the rioters" (Glatt, *Rage and Roll,* 111). I am quite sure he was not tied to a chair.

20. See http://www.luminist.org/archives/wpp.htm.

21. Again, Glatt gives a more lurid account. He claims that "the more militant Motherfuckers went on a rampage after the show, breaking an usher's arm with a metal bar and stabbing a young Puerto Rican boy. The asbestos stage curtain was slashed with a knife, and there were hundreds of dollars worth of damage to equipment" (Glatt, *Rage and Roll,* 113).

22. Wayne Kramer, "Riots I Have Known and Loved," Originally published in "Left of the Dial" online music magazine, No. 4, http://makemyday.free.fr/wk1.htm.

23. Paul Nelson, "The Motherfuckers: Fillmore East vs. The East Village: The Full Report," *Rolling Stone,* February 15, 1969.

24. Was I, as Eric Erikson might say, trapped in unresolved conflicts of the anal stage of development wherein the child masters control of his or her bowels? In this stage:

   > The matter of mutual regulation faces its severest test. If outer control is too rigid or two early training insists on robbing the child of his attempt gradually to control his bowels . . . he will again be faced with a double rebellion and a double defeat. Powerless in his own body (and often fearing his feces as if they were hostile monsters inhabiting his insides) and powerless outside, he will again be forced to seek satisfaction and control either by regression or by false progression. In other words he will return to an earlier, oral control—i.e., by sucking his thumb and becoming whiny and demanding; *or he will become hostile and intrusive, using his feces as ammunition and* pretending

autonomy, an ability to do without anybody to lean on, which
he has by no means really gained.[emphasis added] (Erik Erikson, Childhood and Society, Norton, 1993, p. 82)

25. Nicholas Black Elk as told to John G. Neihardt, *Black Elk Speaks: The Life Story of a Holy Man of the Oglala Sioux* (Lincoln, NE: University of Nebraska Press, 1961).

26. "Our purpose is to abolish the system (call it the Greed Machine, capitalism, the Great Hamburger Grinder, Babylon, Do-Your-Job-ism) and learn to live cooperatively, intelligently, gracefully (call it the New Awareness, anarchism, The Aquarian Age, communism, whatever you wish)," Marvin Garson, "The System Does Not Work," *San Francisco Express-Times*, January 1969, http://www.hippy.com/article-115.html.

27. Alfred Lord Tennyson, "Flower in the Crannied Wall," *A Little Treasury of Great Poetry*, edited by Oscar Williams (New York: Scribner, 1947).

28. Abbie Hoffman, "TWA Never Gets You There on Time," *Revolution for the Hell of It,* The Dial Press, 1968, p. 40.

29. Feminism has had its own critique of the rational/irrational polarity:

> If we listen well to the connotations of "irrational" they are highly charged: we hear overtones of "hysteria" (that disease once supposed to arise in the womb), of "madness" (the *absence* of form.) Thus no attempt need be made to discover a form or a language or a pattern foreign to those which technological reason has already recognized. Moreover, the term "rational" relegates to its opposite term all that it refuses to deal with, and thus ends by assuming itself to be purified of the nonrational, rather than searching to identify and assimilate its own surreal or nonlinear elements. This single error may have mutilated patriarchal thinking—especially scientific and philosophical thinking—more than we yet understand. (Adrienne Rich *Of Women Born,* W.W. Norton & Company: New York, p. 62)

30. "Beauty is "une promesse de Bonheur," Stendhal, *De l'Amour,* enotes.com/ famous quotes, http://history.enotes.com/famous-quotes/beauty-is-only-the-promise-of-happiness quoted in Herbert Marcuse, *One Dimensional Man* (Beacon, 1964), p. 210. Herbert cited the quotation often. It encapsulates his views about the significance of art. (See Douglas Kellner, "Introduction" to *Art and Liberation,*Volume 4 of Herbert Marcuse's Collected Papers, Routledge, 2007, p. 48.)

31. The Black Bloc rhetoric and tactics were very similar to those of the Motherfuckers. The following is a description of one of their actions:

On November 30, several groups of individuals in black bloc attacked various corporate targets in downtown Seattle. Among them were (to name just a few):

—Fidelity Investment (major investor in Occidental Petroleum, the bane of the U'wa tribe in Columbia)

—Bank of America, US Bancorp, Key Bank and Washington Mutual Bank (financial institutions key in the expansion of corporate repression)

—Old Navy, Banana Republic and the GAP (as Fisher family businesses, rapers of Northwest forest lands and sweatshop laborers)

—NikeTown and Levi's (whose overpriced products are made in sweatshops)

—McDonald's (slave-wage fast-food peddlers responsible for destruction of tropical rainforests for grazing land and slaughter of animals)

—Starbucks (peddlers of an addictive substance whose products are harvested at below-poverty wages by farmers who are forced to destroy their own forests in the process)

—Warner Bros. (media monopolists)

—Planet Hollywood (for being Planet Hollywood)

This activity lasted for over 5 hours and involved the breaking of storefront windows and doors and defacing of facades. Slingshots, newspaper boxes, sledge hammers, mallets, crowbars and nail-pullers were used to strategically destroy corporate property and gain access (one of the three targeted Starbucks and Niketown stores were looted). Eggs filled with glass etching solution, paint-balls, and spray-paint were also used.

The black bloc was a loosely organized cluster of affinity groups and individuals who roamed around downtown, pulled this way by a vulnerable and significant storefront and that way by the sight of a police formation. Unlike the vast majority of activists who were pepper-sprayed, tear-gassed and shot at with rubber bullets on several occasions, most of our section of the black bloc escaped serious injury by remaining constantly in motion and avoiding engagement with the police. We buddied up, kept tight and watched each others' backs. Those attacked by federal thugs were un-arrested by quick-thinking and organized members of the black bloc. The sense of solidarity was awe-inspiring." (Infoshop.org http://www.infoshop.org/octo/wto_blackbloc .html)

32. Herbert Marcuse, "A Note on Dialectic," preface to *Reason and Revolution: Hegel and the Rise of Social Theory* (Boston: Beacon Press, 1960), p. xii-xiii.

33. Carolyn Merchant traces the role of science in preparing the world for exploitation back to the sixteenth century:

> Between 1500 and 1700 an incredible transformation took place. A "natural" point of view about the world in which bodies did not move unless activated, either by an inherent organic mover or a "contrary to nature" superimposed "force," was replaced by a non- non-natural non-experiential "log" that bodies move uniformly unless hindered. The "natural" perception of a geocentric earth in a finite cosmos was superseded by the "non-natural" common sense "fact" of a heliocentric infinite universe. . . . Living animate nature died, while dead inanimate money was endowed with life. Increasingly capital and the market would assume the organic attributes of growth, strength, activity, pregnancy, weakness, decay, and collapse obscuring and mystifying the new underlying social relations of production and reproduction that make economic growth and progress possible. Nature, women, blacks, and wage laborers were set on a path towards a new status as "natural" and the human resources for the modern world system. Perhaps the ultimate irony in these transformations with a new name given to them: rationality. (Carolyn Merchant, *The Death of Nature, Women, Ecology and the Scientific Revolution* [New York: Harper and Row, 1983], p. 288)

34. Bill Clinton, Speech At The Signing Ceremony For the North American Free Trade Agreement, September 14, 1993, http://www.craypoe.com/1/historic_docs/speeches/clinton_nafta_speech.html.

35. George Bush, Remarks by the President on Iraq, Cincinnati Museum Center, Cincinnati Union Terminal, Cincinnati, Ohio October 7, 2002, http://www.whitehouse.gov/news/releases/2002/10/20021007-8.html.

36. Arnon Regular "'Road map is a life saver for us,' PM Abbas tells Hamas," *Haaretz*, April 2, 2006, http://www.haaretz.com/hasen/pages/ShArt.jhtml?itemNo=310788&contrassID=2&subContrassID=1&sbSubContrassID=0&listSrc=Y.

37. Vaclav Havel, "The End of the Modern Era," *New York Times*, March 1, 1992, http://www.gse.buffalo.edu/FAS/Bromley/classes/theory/Havel.htm.

38. W. E. B. DuBois, *Black Folk: Then and Now* (New York, 1939), p. 144, quoted in Sterling Stuckey, *Going Through the Storm: The Influence of African American Art in History,* Oxford University Press, 1994, p. 133.

39. "A Television Conversation: James Baldwin, Peregrine Worsthorne, Bryan Magee Encounter/1972," Fred L. Standley, James Baldwin, Louis H. Pratt, and H. Pratt Louis, *Conversations with James Baldwin* (Jackson: University Press of Mississippi, 1989), p. 116.

40. "The Basis of Black Power," Student Nonviolent Coordinating Committee (SNCC) Position Paper, 1966, http://www.hartford-hwp.com/archives/45a/387 .html.

41. Tony Kushner, *Slavs! Thinking About the Longstanding Problems of Virtue and Happiness*, Theater Communications Group, Inc., 1995.